The
GILDED
CAKE

The golden rules
of cake decorating
for metallic cakes

Faye Cahill

www.sewandso.co.uk

Contents

All That Glitters

Cake decorating is about making something sweet and precious. We make cakes to celebrate cherished friends and family and to express our love for them. Metallics are a wonderful way to symbolically show someone that they are treasured. Nothing can beat the prestige of pure edible gold. It will hold the spotlight and turn the glamour up to 'eleven'.

Gold and other metallics can be used on cakes in endless ways. There are many edibles with a brilliant shine and the applications and possibilities for design are limitless. I have tried in this book to include as many different materials and techniques as I can. I am lucky to have a busy cake studio where we work with new designs and techniques on a regular basis. The designs in this book draw on our work in the studio: the cakes we have loved the most and new ideas that have arisen from the working process.

The danger of metallics is to overdo it and end up with something more trashy than refined. There's nothing wrong with gold-on-gold-on-gold, as long as it's done right. The trick is artful application and an eye for design. Sometimes the best use of metallic is to highlight some fine details with a light touch. Sometimes, a liberal use of pearl, gold and glitter will be exactly the luxurious look that's desired.

Here are few things to think about when designing with metallics:

CONTRAST

For example, if I'm using a lot of metallic leaf and highlighting, it may be best to leave the base icing with a matte finish rather than a pearlised one. The shine of metallics will be highlighted when set against a flatter background.

TEXTURE

The texture of metallics can either be flat and shiny like leafing and lustre, or heavy and detailed such as gold painted mouldings. Use texture sparingly and intentionally. I prefer to place sugar flowers against less heavily textured parts of the cake, to avoid a 'messy' feel, and to keep some areas of the cake unadorned to highlight the sharp and beautiful shape.

COMPOSITION

Think about how the eye moves around the cake. Is there a strong focal point or a few smaller elements that lead the eye from one to the next? Careful use of metallic features will help in creating a unified design that's pleasing to look over.

BALANCE

Is the design symmetrical or asymmetric? Symmetrical designs often look more formal and structured; they are perfect for regal and classic styles and work beautifully with metallics. The details should look precise and deliberate. Asymmetric styles are often more relaxed and informal but should still be balanced. For example, the heavy metallic flowers on the Fall Foliage cake are balanced by the delicate 'sunset' airbrushing of copper and gold on the lower tiers and framed by the unadorned upper tiers.

I hope you will enjoy this book and find inspiration for your own cake designs. Thank you for joining me on this fun journey into the world of decorating with metallics!

Recipes

I will leave you to select your favourite cake recipes, but in this book I have used a few things like meringue and ganache in the decoration of the cakes, and so I'm providing you with what I know are good recipes for these.

MERINGUES

Ingredients

- 300g (10½oz) caster (superfine) sugar
- 150g (5½oz) free-range egg white (from about five eggs)
- Flavourings such as cocoa powder, raspberry powder, if required
- Food colouring, if required

METHOD

Pour the egg whites into the bowl of a stand mixer fitted with a whisk attachment. Make sure the bowl is very clean. Whisk on a low speed setting until bubbles start to form, increase to high speed and continue whisking until stiff peaks form (a). You should be able to turn the mixing bowl upside down without the egg white falling out. Add the sugar in large spoonfuls, whisking on high speed after each addition and checking that the mix comes back to stiff peaks each time. Continue to whisk for 5–7 minutes until the peaks are smooth and shiny and if you rub the mix between your fingers, you can't feel any grittiness from undissolved sugar. Add any required colour and flavour to all or part of the mix by gently folding in flavour and/or colour components. Work quickly to avoid flattening the air bubbles. Pipe 'kisses', like peaked blobs about 3.5cm (1⅜in) in size, onto a baking (parchment) paper-lined baking tray or dehydrator tray using a large piping bag fitted with a large round piping nozzle (tip) with an opening of around 12mm (½in). Bake in an oven preheated to 100°C (225°F) for 30–40 minutes until the kisses can be easily lifted from the tray and come away with their bases intact. Meringues can also 'cooked' by drying them in a dehydrator set to around 50°C (110°F) for 8–10 hours. Allow to cool completely.

ROYAL ICING

Ingredients

- 450g (1lb) icing (confectioner's) sugar
- 90g (3¼oz) free-range egg white (from around three eggs)
- Two to three drops acetic acid, or four to five drops white vinegar
- One to two teaspoons glycerine (optional)

METHOD

Ensure all your utensils are very clean and free from grease. Add the egg whites to the mixing bowl of a stand mixer fitted with the paddle attachment. Sift the sugar through a fine sieve, add it to the bowl and stir. Begin mixing at a low speed until the mix is opaque and gluey, then increase to high and mix until stiff peaks form that fall over slightly at the tip. This can take up to 10 minutes or more. Add the acetic acid or vinegar (b) and mix until incorporated. I use the paddle attachment rather than whisk to avoid aerating the icing too much. Over-aerated icing can result in air-pockets and a bubbly finish when the royal is used as a coating and frequent breaks when used for piping. Glycerine may be added at the end: this will help the icing flow smoothly when used for piping and also stop the icing from setting rock hard when it's used to coat cakes.

Meringues stored in an airtight container will keep for up to two weeks.

WHITE CHOCOLATE GANACHE

Ingredients

- 1.5kg (3lb 5oz) white chocolate buttons
- 400ml (14fl oz) double (heavy/pouring) cream
- 45g (1⅝oz) glucose
- 120g (4½oz) unsalted butter

DARK CHOCOLATE GANACHE

Ingredients

- 1.2kg (2lb 10½oz) dark chocolate, broken into small pieces
- 450ml (16fl oz) double (heavy/pouring) cream
- 50g (1¾oz) glucose
- 100g (3½oz) unsalted butter

METHOD

The method for both white and dark chocolate ganache is the same. Place the chocolate and cream in a glass or microwave-proof bowl and microwave on high for approximately 7 minutes until very hot. Stir thoroughly with a wooden spoon until all the lumps melt and the mixture looks smooth (c). This may take 2–3 minutes or more of stirring. Add the butter and glucose and mix until well incorporated. The function of the glucose and butter is to fill the gaps between the molecules of chocolate, which results in a smoother mix and nicer mouth feel. The use of butter also has the effect of tricking the tongue into thinking the taste is less sweet, which is especially important for the white chocolate ganache which can tend to be overly sweet. Refrigerate overnight to set and then bring the ganache to room temperature before use.

Equipment

If you've found that designing cakes has become a bit of a passion, you will no doubt have accumulated a basic toolkit of equipment. These pages show what I use most often. I've divided the items up into categories, so you can see what is needed for each stage.

A. FOR LAYERING, FILLING AND MASKING CAKES FOR A SHARP EDGE FINISH

1. Serrated knife
2. Offset spatula
3. Paring knife
4. Flat scraper with long blade
5. Right-angled scraper or ruler
6. Simple syrup, flavoured with liquor
7. Ruler with millimetres (or 1⁄16s of an inch)
8. Flat palette knife
9. Pastry brush
10. Working board or food board
11. Rigid cake boards such as silver-covered masonite
12. Non-slip mat

B. FOR FONDANT COVERING

13. Rolling pin
14. Modelling tool such as soft blade or tapered end
15. Paring knife
16. Straight edged smoothers
17. Cornflour (cornstarch)
18. Non-slip mat
19. Acupuncture needles
20. Jam (jelly) syrup
21. Acetate buffers

C. FOR DECORATING

22. Silicone moulds
23. Culinary stencil
24. Pasta machine
25. Cake decorator's alcohol (95% ethanol)
26. Scissors
27. Design knife or scalpel
28. Tweezers
29. Edible glaze spray
30. Tissues
31. Artist's paintbrushes, different sizes
32. Edible pen
33. Hot glue gun
34. Pastry brushes
35. Edible marker

D. FOR FLOWER MAKING

36. Florist's wires
37. Florist's tape, Parafilm (plastic) and Floratape (crepe)
38. Cornflour (cornstarch)
39. Petal pad
40. Sugar glue
41. Foam balls
42. Silicone moulds for flower centres
43. Petal and leaf impression mats
44. Petal dusts
45. Cutters including flower, leaf and circles
46. Frilling tool
47. Paintbrushes and fluffy dusting brushes
48. Balling tool
49. Paring knife
50. Small rolling pin

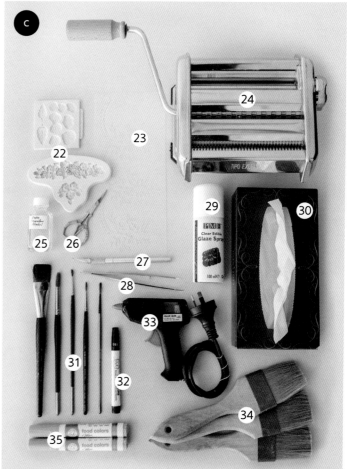
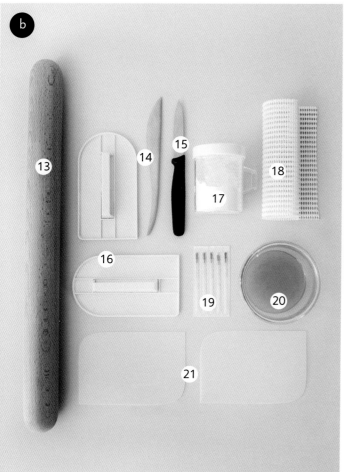
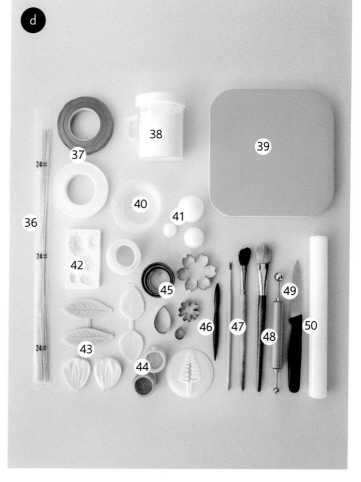

Metallics

I first began using edible gold leaf back in 2006. Although it had long been used to add accents on chocolates and fine desserts, it was not widely applied to larger areas on cakes. Once I tried it, I was hooked. Other coloured metallic leafs can be seen on cakes but, apart from silver leaf, they are not edible. Loose leaf is much trickier than transfer sheets as it takes very gentle handling. I rarely use it but it can have an appealing, softer look than the very polished results you get with transfer sheets.

GOLD AND SILVER LEAF TRANSFER SHEETS

All 24-carat gold and real silver is considered edible and can be found at art stores (remember to ask for transfer sheets!). I prefer to buy from a supplier that has a specified food-grade leaf, including a 23-carat that is a bit less expensive than the 24. In addition to 23-carat gold (a, top left) several alternative shades are now available – 18-carat green-gold (a, top right), 16-carat lemon gold (a, bottom left) and 12-carat white gold (a, bottom right). You can also find food-grade silver leaf in transfer sheet form.

ESTIMATING QUANTITIES OF LEAF

The table below shows the quantities of leaf required for various size tiers, based on a tier height of 12.5cm (5in), and a sheet size of 8 x 8cm (3¼ x 3¼in) for golds and 9.5 x 9.5cm (3¾ x 3¾in) for silver. There can be variation in board size and icing thickness that will affect quantities, but allowance has been made for overlap and wastage.

cake size	no. of sheets, round cake, silver	no. of sheets, round cake, gold	no. of sheets, square cake, silver	no. of sheets, square cake, gold
12.5cm (5in)	6.5	7.5	8	9.5
15cm (6in)	7.5	9	9.5	11.5
18cm (7in)	9	10.5	11.5	13.5
20cm (8in)	10	12	13	15
23cm (9in)	12	13.5	14.5	17
25cm (10in)	13.5	15	15.5	19
28cm (11in)	14	16.5	18	21
30cm (12in)	15	18	19.5	22.5
35.5cm (14in)	17.5	21	22.5	26.5

EDIBLE SILVER DRAGEES

These are one of the shiniest and most metallic of the edible decoratives and are brilliant for replicating beaded fabrics. Dragees (sometimes called cachous) are a hard candy with a polished silver shell. The silver colour is real silver, the same as silver leaf, and these beads usually contain gelatin. The beads are now available in coloured tints for some fun effects. I find that I use the silver variety the most.

Carrot shape (b, top left), flat bead shape (b, top right), baton shape (b, bottom left), rice shape (b, bottom right), pear shape (c, top left), seed shape (c, top right), 2mm (¹⁄₁₆in) sprinkles (c, bottom left), 5mm (¼in) round (c, bottom right)

LUSTRE POWDERS

These are a mineral-based edible colour used to create a pearlised, shimmery or satin effect. They are usually composed of food grade mica and titanium, and edible food colours. Lustres can be combined with high grade alcohol and applied with a brush or an airbrush. They can also be dry dusted onto items with fat content, such as chocolate, or added to wet mixes, such as edible lace or gelatin. Colours include Signature Gold, which I very often use in my designs, but a whole range of powders are available (d), including Pearl White (e).

OTHER MATERIALS

Sanding sugar has larger than normal crystals, the flat faces of which reflect the light giving a sparkly appearance (f). It will not melt when subject to heat and is available in many colours. Sanding sugar can be used to simulate water and snow, and is also used to embellish cookies or even as a textured finish over a whole tier of cake.

Jimmies are a bead-like edible that can have a pearlised finish (g). They are similar to sprinkles, and are smaller and more delicate than dragees. They can be used to create fine beaded patterns, although this can be very time-consuming to apply. However, it is a very effective way to add detail into a lace design.

Edible glitter is made from minerals such as mica, and is similar to craft glitter in appearance and texture (h). The particles are larger than those in lustre so it is not suitable for airbrushing. Edible glitter is normally applied with a brush to a surface made sticky with sugar glue or piping gel. The small particles can shed, but a spray of edible glaze will help keep them in place. Many glitters are food touch approved, rather than edible, and glittered items should be removed before serving. Check the labelling carefully before using glitter on cakes.

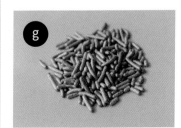

Metallic Techniques

Painting

In my opinion, hand painting is one of the best techniques to elevate a cake from ordinary to special. It's easy to customise painted cakes to match a theme or motif, and you won't need any extra equipment, so it's also very cost effective. Most commonly I will paint using high grade alcohol combined with petal dusts, liquid or paste food colours and edible metallic lustres.

LARGER AREAS AND COLOUR WASHES

Colour washes can be anything from muted tinges to bold neons. They add an arty edge to cakes and can be used to create striking blocks of colour as well as subtle ombre gradients. You can mix your own colours or add lustre for a metallic finish.

For covering large areas, add a drop or two of liquid colour into cake decorator's alcohol (95%) and paint using a large brush. Try to avoid having too much liquid in the brush, unless you are trying to achieve drip lines.

If creating an ombre look, start with the palest colour and gradually add more drops of liquid colour as you paint the deeper tones (a). Too much liquid colour in the alcohol can cause it to go streaky. Paint quickly and don't go over the same area too many times.

Metallics can also be painted as solid colour washes or brushed lines. Use a thicker mix of lustre and alcohol and paint with a large brush. The visible brushed lines can look great painted either horizontally (b) or vertically (c). They can be painted onto fondant and also work beautifully as a finish on a semi-frosted style cake.

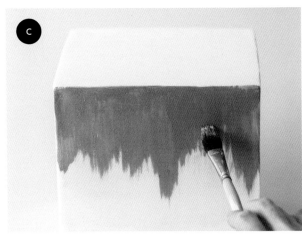

TRANSFERRING A PATTERN

Before you can start to decorate, you'll need to transfer your design onto a fondant-covered cake. Use a fine fabric such as chiffon or netting and an edible pen to trace the design onto the cake before adding colour and embellishment.

1. Trace your design onto a piece of fine fabric using an edible pen (d). Move the fabric away from the original template to ensure that you have transferred the full design (e).

2. Pin the fabric to the cake and trace using the edible pen (f). The design will transfer onto the fondant through the fabric.

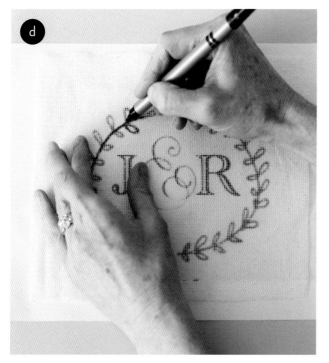

Hand painting can add a delicate and pretty touch or designer style. Hand-painted designs always get a few more 'wows' and are easier to customise than stencils or moulds.

CALLIGRAPHY AND FINE LINE PAINTING

Painting fine lines onto cakes requires a steady hand, but is quite a straightforward technique. It allows you to add personal touches, such as your own unique motifs and designs, or even elaborate monograms, names and dates with calligraphy.

1. Mix lustre with alcohol (a). For fine painting, it's better to use vodka or a similar alcohol with 40-70% alcohol rather than 95%. The slight stickiness of the lower grade alcohol will 'set' the painting to prevent smudging or shedding of the lustre powder. Use a thicker mix of paint for better coverage.

2. Paint the design using a fine brush with long bristles (b). The longer brush will make it easier to achieve long, smooth lines. Try not to go over the same area multiple times or it may become streaky. If it does, allow it to dry before painting over the streaks.

Support your hand while painting to achieve more precise detailing.

FIXING MISTAKES

If you make a mistake, just follow this simple technique to remove any excess paint.

Paint over the area with a little water (c) and quickly blot with a tissue (d). You may need to repeat this several times to remove the mistake (e), but try not to use too much water or leave it on for long or it will dissolve the fondant and create a hole.

If the mistake comes off quickly the correction should not be very visible, but if needed you can dust a little cornflour (cornstarch) onto the area to remove any shine. Then repaint the blotted area to correct the mistake (f).

Leafing

Many decorators get nervous about using gold and silver leaf, however it only takes a couple of practices to become competent with the transfer sheets, and then it becomes a fast way to add a luxurious feel to a cake. Of course the material cost needs to be factored into the cake price. Silver leaf is relatively inexpensive, but the golds can add a lot to the cost of producing the cake.

WORKING WITH GOLD AND SILVER LEAF

I generally use transfer sheets when working with gold or silver leaf on cake. The leaf is lightly attached to a backing sheet, which makes it easy to transfer onto the cake. Store the leaf in closed packets at cool room temperature or sealed well in the refrigerator. If the leaf becomes too warm, the wax of the backing sheet can meld to the leaf and cause it to go on very unevenly. For the number of sheets of leaf you will need, please see the table in Metallics at the beginning of this book.

When wetting the cake, you are looking for the surface to be evenly tacky. Too wet and you are likely to get large cracks and imperfections, too dry and the leaf will not adhere. Whenever using water on a cake, try not to leave it on for too long or it will eat into the surface.

APPLYING A FULL TIER OF METALLIC LEAF

Many of my multi-tier designs combine several different patterns and finishes. The full tier of metallic leaf is a popular choice to add in the mix. Most commonly I apply the leaf to the sides only and leave the top of the cake uncovered. This is a design choice, I like the way the leaf highlights the sharp edge of the cake. It can be taken over onto the top surface easily if needed.

1. To get started, wet an area of the tier larger than a sheet of leaf, using a soft paintbrush dipped in water. Only wet the area you will be applying the leaf to, and make sure there are no dry patches (a).

2. Use a tissue to blot off the excess water. Press the tissue flat against the side of the cake (b). Scrunching and blotting takes off the moisture in a less consistent way. Remove the tissue and quickly move on to the leaf application after wetting. Don't wet too large an area or it will either dry out before you get to it, or melt the fondant producing a rough texture. On the other hand, if you are looking for a more textured finish you could deliberately leave the water on for longer before blotting.

3. For a really sharp line at the top of the cake, try to line up the top edge of the leaf with the top edge of the cake. Hold the sheet taut and press the leaf onto the tacky fondant (c). Rub over the entire sheet with your finger or a soft fluffy brush.

4. Slowly peel away the backing sheet (d). If there are some areas that have not adhered well, you can put the backing sheet down again and give an extra rub over. After removing the sheet, the first thing to look for is any 'puffy' areas where the leaf is not completely adhered to the cake. Again, take a backing sheet and give an extra rub over these areas to bed down the leaf.

5. Work around the tier, overlapping each new sheet by 5mm (¼in) (e). You don't need to wet the previous applied leaf, but after adding the new piece take a backing sheet and place it over the seam, then give an extra rub to smooth over the join.

6. Fill in the lower part of the tier using sheets cut down to the required size with scissors (f). You can either try to fill right down to the base if there will be no trim, or be a little less precise if there is a margin for a trim or ribbon to be added. If the leaf is intended to go right down to the base, it can work well to again line up one of the straight edges of the leaf with the bottom edge of cake. To do this, you will need to trim the backing sheet away at that edge.

7. If there are defects that need to be covered, wet and blot that area – it can be harder to get a tiny area to the ideal tacky stage – then either cut a shape to cover the area you need, or 'blot' just a small section from a larger sheet (g). Only the area that touches the cake will adhere, the rest will come away with the backing sheet and can be used again. Take a full backing sheet, cover the repair and give an extra rub over. If there is a very large area of imperfection, you can cover with a whole new sheet. At the end of the process, if there are visible flaky bits of leaf, they can be dusted away with a soft fluffy brush. If possible leave this until the next day as the brush can cause defects in the leaf before the fondant has fully dried from having water applied.

For a more distressed and rustic look, you can rub and smudge the leafing in a few areas to create defects or even touch the sheet of leaf before applying so that some leaf is removed and will leave an open area on the fondant. Note that, on a display cake, silver leaf will start to discolour after a few weeks in the light, turning a light gold colour. Gold leaf will retain its colour over time.

CREATING A BAND OF LEAF

A band of leaf can be a lighter way to incorporate a metallic element into a design. Where a full tier of gold or silver might be a bit visually heavy, a band can be more suitable for upper tiers. And a fine band can make a delicate finishing trim.

1. Use a cardboard collar, which has been cut to the required size, around the cake and use that as a template to draw a line with an edible pen (a).

2. Lay a sheet of leaf face down on top of an empty backing sheet. Use your template and a cocktail stick (toothpick) to score lines to the width of the cardboard, allowing about 2mm (1/16in) extra to make sure the pen line on the cake will be covered (b).

3. Cut the sheet of leaf along the scored lines (c). You want to try to achieve nice straight edges so that they will line up neatly with the pen line.

4. Wet and blot the area inside the line (see Applying a Full Tier of Metallic Leaf, steps 1 and 2). Apply the cut sheet and rub over to transfer the leaf (d).

5. Continue around the cake, overlapping each new piece of leaf by about 5mm (1/4in). If the leaf lands above the line and adheres, gently scrape it back with a sharp paring knife. If it lands too low and there is a gap under the line, cut a sliver off a new sheet, wet and blot the area to be filled and apply the new piece. Use an empty backing sheet to rub over the join (e).

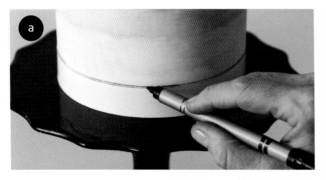

STENCILLING OVER LEAF

Applying a stencil over a tier of gold or silver can be nerve-wracking! It's not uncommon for some of the leaf to be pulled away when the stencil is removed. To minimise the chance of this happening, leave the cake overnight after leafing before stencilling. The leaf will be bedded down and set in place better. For more detail on stencilling, see the Golden Regency cake, step 2.

1. Pin the stencil to the cake using two pins at each end. Make sure it's firm and tight against the cake, then add masking tape to line up with the tier edge (f). This will prevent the royal icing from bleeding out onto the top surface of the cake. This is particularly important when stencilling with coloured icing.

2. Using royal icing that is of a fairly thick consistency to minimise bleeding, spread it thinly across the stencil with a palette knife, using firm pressure (g).

3. Use a large plastic scraper to remove the excess royal icing. Scrape firmly and quickly across the stencil a few times (h). Don't take too long or overwork it, or the royal icing will become powdery. For a finer look, scrape back quite hard; or if you prefer a bit more texture to the design, go a little easier on the scraping. Take the pins out and scrape over that area with the palette knife before removing the stencil. Alternatively, the pin holes can be covered later by piping a dot of royal on them, and flattening each dot with a damp brush.

4. After removing the stencil, check for defects. There can be areas where the royal icing has bled a little and it may be possible to scrape unwanted icing back with a cocktail stick (toothpick) or damp brush (i). If there are thicker areas that have a ragged edge, pat them down with a damp paintbrush.

If there are areas of the design where the leaf has come away when the stencil was removed, you might choose whether or not to make a repair. Usually smaller defects are not very noticeable in a complex pattern, but for significant defects it can be a delicate job of cutting very small pieces of leaf to fill small areas between the royal icing motifs.

GILDING WAFER PAPER

Decorations made with gilded wafer paper have that 'wow, how is that edible?' effect. The whole sheet can be covered in one colour of leaf, of course, or you can have fun with a mixed metallic like this one. Gilded wafer paper can be single-sided or double-sided depending on the intended use. The smooth side of the paper is considered the front and the rougher side is the back.

1. To add leaf to wafer paper, you need to use piping gel rather than water, as water would instantly melt the wafer. Paint the gel thinly onto the wafer paper with a wide paintbrush (a).

2. Apply the leaf to the wafer paper, rub over the backing sheet and then peel it away (b). See the method described in Applying a Full Tier of Metallic Leaf, but use piping gel rather than water.

3. Using different types of metallic leaf creates a variety of effects. Use silver leaf, white gold and lemon gold leaf to cover the majority of the wafer paper. Then create a graduated effect by adding some green gold between the existing golds (c). Offcuts with natural edges are ideal, or use a 'dabbing' technique so only some of the leaf comes off and you can avoid including any hard straight edges.

4. Use the 'dabbing' technique again to add flecks of different coloured leaf as highlights (d). Try adding some 23-carat gold onto the silver area and some silver onto the 23-carat area to create interest. Use a small brush lightly dipped in a little piping gel, and gently dab on a sheet of leaf to produce the small painterly flecks.

5. If needed, cover the gilded wafer paper with a sheet of silicone paper and give it a good firm rub to bed down any flaky areas (e).

6. A spray of edible glaze will make the paper easier to handle (f), especially if it is to be cut into strips. Leave it overnight to dry. For double-sided gilding, spray one side and allow to dry then turn over onto silicone paper and spray the other side and allow to dry. It's preferable to gild the paper the day before using it, even if you don't finish it off with edible spray, as the gel makes the paper sticky and hard to handle straight away.

The 'dabbing' technique works just as well on a fondant or ganache cake as it does on wafer paper, and is a great way to dress up a simpler style soft finish cake such as a fresh flower design.

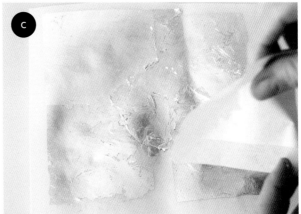

GILDING AN APPLIQUÉ SHAPE

It can be easier to gild an appliqué decoration before it is applied to the cake. This is the method I use if I want the cut edge of the shape to remain free of metallic. It's particularly effective on dark colours.

1. Roll out your fondant and cut the shape required, by hand or with a cutter (g). Leave the excess fondant around the shape.

2. Wet the shape and a small area outside the cut using a paintbrush dipped in water, and blot it with a tissue (h).

3. Apply leaf to cover the shape and then remove the backing sheet (i).

4. Remove the shape and gently rub over the edges with a finger to smooth them down (j).

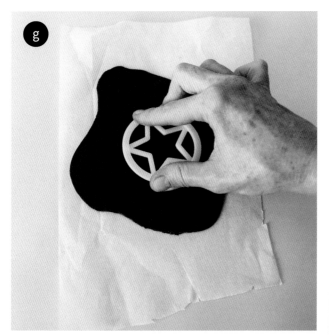

Be careful when transferring the shape onto the cake as it will crack easily with movement. I sometimes support it on an acetate smoother while transferring it onto the cake.

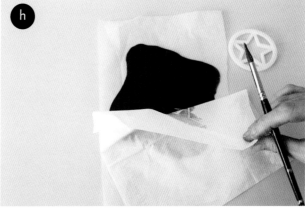

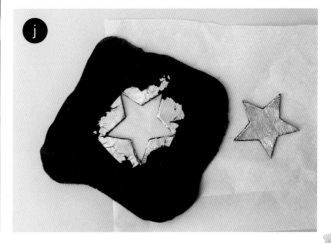

Airbrushing

I tend to favour hand techniques over technologies like airbrushing, however there are some cases where I find it invaluable. If I'm applying a full tier lustre finish I'll always favour using pastry brushes and alcohol wash (see Applying Lustre) as I like the softness of visible brush strokes. Where I find airbrushing most useful is to create a gradient or ombre effect, or to deepen and improve the finish of deep coloured fondant, and to quickly add a metallic finish to a stencilled design.

WORKING WITH AN AIRBRUSH

There are two types of airbrush guns – single and double action. With the single action gun, you pull back the lever to start the flow of both air and paint. The double action gun has a more customisable mechanism: pushing down on the lever starts the flow of air and then pulling back gets the paint flowing. Both the air and paint flow can be managed by the finger pressure that you use. I use a double action gun, however, both types are fine for the simple techniques we are describing here.

Work in a well ventilated area and use a dust mask while airbrushing. Best practice is to have an extractor fan to remove the overspray from the airbrush. The residue can settle on surfaces in the room leaving a film of colour pigment. You can use either a plain airbrush colour or an edible paint made by mixing lustre powder and cake decorator's alcohol (95%). After finishing an airbrush job, never forget to clean the gun as dried paint will cause blockages. You can tell when the gun is blocked because either no paint will come out or it will come out in rough splatters rather than a fine mist. Clean the gun after each use or if it becomes blocked by running through plain water and spraying with full force into a cup or sink. Repeat with more water until the water runs completely clear. To completely clean any blockages disassemble the gun and clean all parts individually, paying particular attention to the needle and wiping it thoroughly with a damp cloth to remove any build up of paint or lustre.

Some lustres cannot be airbrushed, particularly those with larger particles designed to give a sparkly look. Usually no warning will be marked on the packet, but if your airbrush becomes blocked repeatedly when using a certain colour, then another method of application would be better. Also bear in mind that unlike the lustre and alcohol mix, plain airbrush colours are water based and need to be applied with a light touch.

CREATING AN OMBRE EFFECT

1. When airbrushing a lustre powder, it needs to be diluted with plenty of alcohol or the gun will quickly become blocked. Use a ratio of one part lustre to 10 parts cake decorator's alcohol (95%), although vodka or other white spirit may be substituted without any problems. Mix the quantity required for the job in a cup or bowl and add a little into the airbrush hopper (a).

2. With the cake on a turntable, begin spraying colour onto the cake (b). If you are using a single action gun, start the flow of paint while pointing away from the cake then gently move the spray onto the cake. If you start spraying while the gun is close to the cake, it's likely to cause a concentrated 'splat' of paint. With the double action gun, press down to start the air and then very gently pull back to start the paint. Use broad horizontal strokes and spin the cake on the turntable, working evenly.

3. To create a gradient, start with the lightest colour and fill the whole area to be coloured. It will take several passes of the airbrush to make the colour solid: work over the cake sides using horizontal strokes, using fewer strokes right at the top to create a lighter tone and a gradual transition to the uncoloured area (c).

4. Next add the deeper colour to the lower part of the cake, using the same even horizontal strokes. Again, use a lighter touch at the top of the new colour to create a smooth transition of tone (d). Gradients can be created either in lustre colours mixed with alcohol as here, or using plain airbrush colours.

5. One thing to keep in mind with airbrushing is that it can be hard to rectify any mistakes. For example, if you get a smudge or touch the surface before the paint is dry, it's very hard to repair the defect in a way that it will be invisible. Usually you will have to make a choice of whether to leave the mistake visible or alter the design to cover it. Minimise handling of airbrushed cakes until the paint is set, and be careful not to drop any water or colour onto an airbrushed cake.

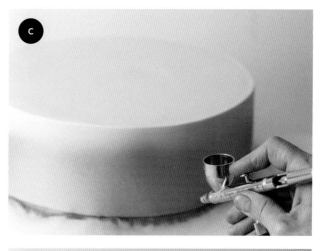

DEEPENING FONDANT COLOUR

1. Fondant cakes covered in strong and dark colours benefit greatly from an airbrush finish. I love the richness and depth it gives the cake – the appearance becomes almost velvety.

2. Sometimes you might be applying a single colour such as black or red, so you can pour it into the airbrush straight out of the bottle. In the case of this navy the colour is a combination of two parts blue to one part each of black and purple. Make sure that you mix enough colour for the entire job (a).

3. Work in smooth strokes around the cake. For a little tier, like this one, you can use vertical strokes and rotate the cake on the turntable as you work around the sides (b). You want the paint to coat the cake completely and work up a deep colour, so keep going over the same area until the desired colour is achieved. If an area becomes too saturated with paint, droplets will form on the surface, which may even turn into runs and drips.

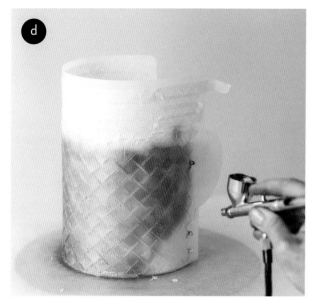

HIGHLIGHTING A STENCILLED EFFECT

1. Stencils can look amazing highlighted in metallics, really adding that something special to take your cake design to the next level. I always used to paint the lustre on the stencil after it was dry. It's extremely time consuming to do it that way, and it's not unusual to have a few mistakes and drips during the painting process. The advantage of this method is that you can paint both the main pattern surface and the tiny edge area that gives the stencil its depth. However, my advice is to airbrush after applying the stencil texture with royal icing (see Leafing: Stencilling Over Leaf for how to apply the stencil effect). It's much quicker to airbrush on the lustre before removing the stencil. Use the same ratio of lustre and alcohol as described in Creating an Ombre Effect and airbrush over the entire face of the stencil. Mask the areas above the height of the cake tier and also at the sides where the stencil finishes to prevent overspray from landing on the non-stencilled areas of the cake (c).

2. Airbrush with your chosen metallic colour in smooth horizontal strokes (d).

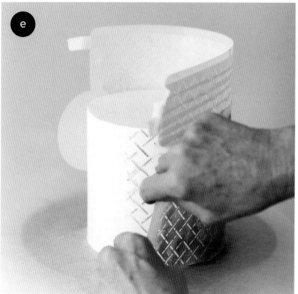

3. Remove the stencil carefully immediately after airbrushing (e), then wait a few minutes till the section of stencil effect just applied is dry and the royal icing is firm enough, before moving on to the next section. Wash and thoroughly dry the stencil before applying it to the next area. The masking will usually stay in place during the washing process.

4. With this method of colouring a stencil, only the front surface will be coloured. The tiny edge will only be revealed when the stencil is pulled away and this will remain in the base colour of the royal icing, in this case, white. Airbrushing is a very efficient way to highlight a stencil such as this lattice which would be a painstaking task to paint by hand (f).

Applying lustre

Edible lustre is a very desirable finish on custom cakes. It softens the look, allows for beautiful subtle colour tints and catches the light wonderfully. Lustre can add a feel of luxury, romance or glamour to a cake and does not take long to apply. I prefer the look of painted lustre to airbrushed as the slight visible brush marks impart a softer and more handmade feel, unlike the somewhat artificial effect of an airbrushed finish.

CREATING A LUSTRE FINISH

Start by assembling the materials that you will need: edible lustre, cake decorator's alcohol (95%), and two or three pastry brushes around 7.5cm (3in) wide, with natural bristle not synthetic.

1. For white and pale tints, first cover the cake in white fondant (see General Techniques: Covering); for strong colours, the base fondant is better tinted to a similar shade as the lustre you plan to use. Place the required amount of lustre into a bowl (a). One tablespoon is usually enough to finish a three tier cake with two coats of lustre.

2. Add cake decorator's alcohol to the powder. The proportion is roughly one tablespoon of lustre to a quarter of a cup (60ml/2fl oz) of alcohol. It should be very fluid, not thick and paste-like (b). White spirits such as vodka will not work for this brush technique: the surface will become sticky. The 95% alcohol works because it will evaporate quickly and not add moisture to the cake.

3. Place the cake on a decorating turntable. If the cake is more than one tier and all tiers will be lustred the same colour, then the cake should be stacked (see General Techniques: Dowelling & Stacking) before applying lustre. Work on one tier at a time from the top to the bottom. Apply the wet mix to the entire top tier with a wide pastry brush (c), working quickly so the lustre can be polished before the alcohol dries.

If the dry brush becomes saturated and clogged up with lustre, either switch to a fresh clean brush or scrub the brush on a clean tea towel or kitchen paper before continuing.

Sometimes the alcohol can evaporate quickly and the mixture will become too thick. This can result in clumps of lustre remaining on the cake surface. These are easily removed by flicking the brush from side to side to sweep them away, however to avoid wasting the product it's better to prevent this by working quickly and making sure your paint is very fluid. Add more alcohol from time to time if needed.

4. Switch to a dry brush and buff the surface until the lustre is dry and any brush marks disappear. Use horizontal strokes across the top surface and then spin the cake on the turntable while holding the brush against it to polish the side (d). Keep the brush level so that any visible brush strokes will be in straight lines. Work from the top of the tier and then move the brush down and work a section at a time until you reach the bottom.

5. Repeat the process for the next tier by applying the wet mix and then switching back to the dry brush and buffing till smooth. The top surface of the tiers is done with a spinning motion (e) and the sides as before. After all tiers are finished with one coat, go back to the top and apply a second coat. There is no need to wait before painting the second coat as the alcohol will have already been brushed until dry. Most cakes will need two coats, even for white lustre on white fondant, the finish will be more opaque and perfect with two coats. If after two coats the tint needs to be adjusted or the finish is not perfect, then you can add more. Beware of over-doing it though, because too many coats may result in a heavy, powdery look.

ADDING INTEREST TO A LUSTRE FINISH

It's sometimes desirable to add interest to the lustre detailing by using an ombre gradient of a darker coloured lustre at the base of the bottom tier. In this example, I have used taupe and blended it into the white lustre.

1. Start by adding the taupe lustre powder and alcohol to a bowl, and mixing as before (a).

2. The cake has already been finished with two coats of white lustre, so the taupe can be brushed over the lower part of the bottom tier (b) and then polished with a dry brush.

Any excess lustre paint can be kept for future use. Either place in a lidded container to preserve both the lustre and the alcohol, or allow the alcohol to evaporate and store the extra lustre as a dry powder. The lustre may be re-used in the same form or added to another mix and colour adjusted for the new job.

3. Create a mid tone by mixing taupe and white lustres together (c).

4. Paint a band of the lighter colour above the taupe section (d), then again polish with a dry brush. For ombre cakes, having a few spare clean brushes will help a lot.

5. Apply a second coat of both taupe and the lighter mix and buff until dry (e). On the second coat, the colours will start to blend more for a more seamless gradient.

To change the tint of a lustre, you can mix together different colours of lustre, add white to lighten the tone, or incorporate non-lustre pigments such as petal dust or liquid/airbrush colours. If using a liquid or airbrush colour, use only a drop or two – any more and the water content can cause streaks and uneven tone. Paste and gel colours are not suitable for adding to a lustre paint.

Cake Projects

Imperial Gold

Topped with a shiny gold bow, this sleek gilded and glazed three-tier cake is sure to make a lasting impression with its bold metallic central tier and contrasting colour scheme. Tailored lines with sharp and structured details make it suitable for a celebration for a man or stronger styling themes.

Materials

- Three round black fondant-covered cakes in the following sizes, all prepared on tier boards with a 16mm (⅝in) drilled hole through the centre: 10cm (4in) diameter by 10cm (4in) tall, 15cm (6in) diameter by 10cm (4in) tall, and 20cm (8in) diameter by 12.5cm (5in) tall. The bottom tier should be embossed shortly after covering while the fondant is still soft.

- Three 25cm (10in) cake boards, 10mm (⅜in) thick

- 30cm (12in) length of 12mm (½in) dowel

- Edible glaze paint

- Edible glaze spray

- Gold leaf, 23- or 24-carat, 25 transfer sheets

- Edible beads: square, macaroni, 5mm (¼in) pearls and 4mm (⁵⁄₃₂in) silver balls

- Four black glass drawer pulls

- Edible lustre powder (Faye Cahill Cake Design Lustre), Graphite Black and Regency Gold

- Cake decorator's alcohol (95%)

- CK Products Diamond Large Impression Mat (embossing sheet)

- Cake smoother

- Wafer paper, one A4 (US letter) sheet

- Hot glue gun

- Piping gel

- Royal icing

- Black velvet ribbon, 5mm (¼in) width, 85cm (33½in)

1. The faux cake stand is integrated into the structure for this cake. To create the base, secure the three 25cm (10in) cake boards together with hot glue to create a platform around 3cm (1¼in) deep. Drill a 12mm (½in) hole through the centre and secure a 30cm (12in) length of 12mm (½in) dowel with hot glue. Drill four small holes about 1cm (⅜in) in from the edges and screw in the glass drawer pulls to create feet (a). Cover the timber platform in black fondant using piping gel to adhere. This is best done at least a day before decorating, or even earlier if possible.

If you don't have a quilting embosser, the lines can be scored using an angled ruler and scriber tool.

2. Secure an embossing sheet to the bottom tier with pins and use a cake smoother to press in the quilted lines (b). Emboss only the top two rows of diamonds and then scribe a vertical line from the lower point of the diamond down to the base of the cake using a right angle as a guide. Pearlise the bottom tier with Graphite Black lustre (see Metallic Techniques: Applying Lustre).

3. Stack all three tiers onto the prepared cake stand using suitable supports and royal icing to secure the tiers together. Apply gold leaf to the sides of the middle tier (see Metallic Techniques: Leafing). Leave some cracks and defects so that the black fondant shows though for a slightly distressed look. Apply edible glaze paint with a large brush to the top tier, top surface of the middle tier and the cake stand. Trim the top and middle tiers with the black velvet ribbon, securing the overlap at the back of the cake with hot glue (see General Techniques: Finishing). Trim the top and bottom edge of the cake stand with the velvet ribbon.

4. Apply piping gel to the quilted lines using a fine paintbrush and add edible square beads, long 'macaroni' beads, white pearls and small silver balls as shown (c). The beads will adhere better if the fondant is still a little soft. Press the beads against the fondant firmly to secure them well. Highlight the small silver beads with a mix of Regency Gold edible lustre and alcohol (d).

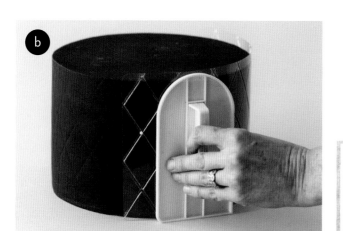

The edible beads should be added on the same day that the cake is covered. The beads will look nicer if pressed into the fondant slightly and will also be better adhered.

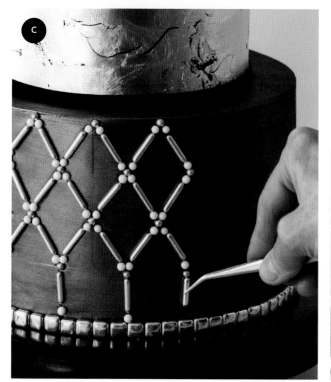

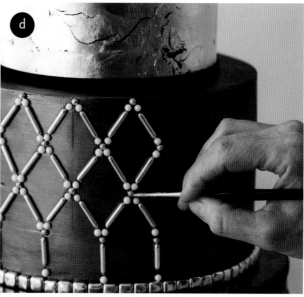

5. Apply gold leaf to a 21 x 30cm (8¼ x 11¾in) sheet of wafer paper (see Metallic Techniques: Leafing). If using the same sheet for both the bow and the lines on the top tier, apply the gold to both sides of the paper. Spray one side with edible glaze and allow to dry, then spray the other side. Leave overnight if possible. Cut two 5mm (¼in) and two 3mm (⅛in) strips lengthways (e).

6. Apply one of the 5mm (¼in) strips across the top edge of the top tier so that the joins are at the side or back. If the glaze is still tacky, you may not need any glue, but if it is fully dry, then apply a thin line of piping gel before attaching. Use a second strip to finish the top band, leaving small overlaps at the joins. Secure the overlaps with piping gel. Add the 3mm (⅛in) strip below the top band with a space of around 3mm (⅛in) between the two bands (f).

7. Cut 12mm (½in) strips lengthways from the gilded wafer paper for the bow. Take six strips that are 22.5cm (9in) long and form into figure eight shapes, using gel to adhere (g). Make three more that are 20cm (8in) in length and one single loop that is around 6.5cm (2½in) long and 2cm (¾in) wide.

8. Stack the loops, using piping gel to glue them together, giving a firm press with each addition (h). Use the six longest pieces for the outside loops and the smaller ones to fill in the middle. Use the small loop as the final piece in the centre to hide the joins underneath.

IMPERIAL GOLD GIFT BOX

Create a sweet gift for someone special featuring a 'bow-tie' variation of the wafer bow. This petit-fours sized mini cake has been covered in black fondant and set on a small square of the gilded and glazed wafer paper.

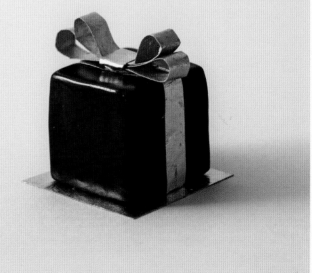

Mademoiselle Meringue

This French-style meringue tower cake would make the sweetest centrepiece for a bridal shower, high afternoon tea or sophisticated birthday party. Touches of gold lustre and a decorative floral border add a hint of elegance to its striking, colourful appearance.

Materials

- One round taupe fondant-covered cake, 20cm (8in) diameter by 10cm (4in) tall, prepared on a tier board

- Taupe fondant-covered foam cone, 25cm (10in) tall

- Taupe royal icing, 250g (9oz)

- Meringue mixture (see Recipes)

- Freeze-dried raspberry powder

- Whole freeze-dried raspberries

- Dried edible flowers, such as fuchsia and rose petal

- Fresh berries, such as blackberries and raspberries

- Cocoa powder

- Edible lustre powder (Faye Cahill Cake Design Lustre), Regency Gold

- Cake decorator's alcohol (95%)

- Pink and brown gel or paste food colours

- Katy Sue Designs Pansies Silicone Mould

- Piping nozzles (tips), Wilton no.32, no. 3 and a large round nozzle (tip), plus piping bags

- Royal icing

1. Place the fondant-covered cone onto the centre of your fondant-covered cake. The covering on the cone can be less perfect as it will be concealed. Wrap a strip of baking (parchment) paper around the covered cake, make a mark where it joins and unwrap to see the area of the cake side. Fold in half, then into quarters and then fold again so that you have eight segments that are each approximately 8cm (3⅛in) wide. Unfold and wrap back around the cake, making a pin mark at the top edge where each fold is (a).

2. Use a pansy mould, or other suitable floral mould, to make eight sets of flowers and leaves with taupe fondant (b). Attach flowers and leaves to the side of the cake using piping gel to secure (c). Push firmly to ensure that they are well adhered.

3. Add a dot each of brown and pink gel colours to royal icing to create a pale taupe colour. Transfer the royal icing into a piping bag and with a Wilton no.32 piping nozzle (tip) held at about 30 degrees to the cake surface, pipe a shell border around the base. Squeeze your piping bag to build up a suitable sized 'blob' and pull slowly away in the direction the border is going, releasing the pressure as you do. Repeat to create a row of shells all around the cake, each one just covering the 'tail' of the one before (d).

4. Using a no.3 round tip, pipe two dropped scallop lines between each flower (e). Start by attaching the piped line next to one flower, then squeeze out a line, letting it drop into a neat scallop before attaching at the other side. Allow to dry for at least 10 minutes before painting

5. Using a mixture of Regency Gold lustre powder and alcohol, paint the pansies and dropped lines (f). Use a thicker consistency of paint that is still thin enough to allow the paint to flow slightly around the shape to give maximum coverage.

Unless the cake is really soft, dowel supports should not be required for the meringue tower, but do use a small cardboard cake board or circle of baking (parchment) paper so that the base of the foam cone does not come into direct contact with the fondant on the top of the tier to be served.

6. Split a meringue mixture (see Recipes) in half. Leave one half white and add freeze-dried raspberry powder to the other half. Then divide the flavoured mix in two, and colour one of these smaller batches with light pink and the other with a deeper raspberry pink. Fill piping bags with the white, pale pink and dark pink meringue mixtures and cut the tip to give a 1cm (⅜in) opening.

7. Prepare a separate piping bag with a large round nozzle (tip) approximately 12mm (½in) in diameter. Create three lines of meringue inside this piping bag by piping a line from near the tip to the outer opening. Pipe smaller lines of the two pink shades first and then fill with plenty of white (g). Lay a sheet of baking (parchment) paper onto a dehydrator tray or baking tray, and pipe 'kisses' of meringue around 3.5cm (1½in) in diameter and height (h). Sprinkle with crumbled freeze-dried raspberries.

8. Create chocolate meringues using the same method, but adding cocoa powder to colour and flavour the pale chocolate colour and some additional brown gel paste colour for the darker shade. Sprinkle the meringues with cocoa powder before baking or dehydrating (i). Make 60 of each of the chocolate and pink meringue kisses. Apply edible gold leaf to around 25 of the meringues, using piping gel to adhere (j) (see Metallic Techniques: Leafing).

9. Use an offset spatula to apply a band of taupe royal icing around the base of the cone. Arrange the meringues in rings, starting at the base of the cone (k). Add a couple of rows at a time, before spreading more royal icing and continuing the process until the whole cone is covered.

10. Attach dried edible flowers, such as fuchsia and rose petals, and whole freeze-dried raspberries between the meringues using piped dots of taupe royal icing if needed. Add some fresh raspberries and blackberries around the base. Mix edible gold lustre with alcohol and brush lightly onto the blackberries to add highlights (l).

Add a tablespoon of glycerine to the royal icing to prevent it from setting rock hard. This will ensure that the meringues are easier to remove and serve.

LEMON CURD TARTS

Simple lemon tarts are transformed into decadent desserts with the addition of little meringue kisses. These luxurious teatime treats have been decorated with a dried fuchsia and fleck of gold leaf. They're best served with fresh berries or berry sorbet.

Artful Appliqué

Inspired by couture fashion detailing, this cake is a boho beauty.
Relaxed yet glamorous, it's the layering of design elements and
organic composition that are the keys to nailing this look. One bonus
is that due to the slightly distressed and random appearance of the
metallic leafing, the application does not have to be perfect.

Materials

- One round white fondant-covered cake, 15cm (6in) diameter by 10cm (4in) tall, prepared on a tier board

- White fondant icing, 500g (1lb 2oz)

- Flexible lace, fishnet pattern, about one third of a sheet

- Royal icing, 100g (3⅓oz)

- Gumpaste, 50g (1¾oz)

- Cutters: small four-petal blossom and tiny leaf

- Embosser, lace or other pattern

- Balling tool and petal pad

- 6mm (¼in) hole punch

- Wafer paper, less than one third of a sheet

- White lustre powder

- Gold leaf, green gold leaf, lemon gold leaf and silver leaf, one transfer sheet of each

- Edible pearls, 10mm (½in) and 5mm (¼in)

- Silver dragees: about 12 carrot-shaped, nine pear-shaped, 20 seed-shaped, 40 rice-shaped, one button-shaped and one 8mm (⅜in) round

- Piping gel

1. First apply the flexible lace to the cake in the areas where the metallic leafing will be. This will give the leafing a subtle texture resembling fish scales. Work over a small area at a time and cover around two thirds of the top surface. Extend some more down the side of the cake to the right of the centre. Brush water onto the surface of the cake in the area that you will apply your flexible lace. Blot with tissue to remove excess water, then lay down your piece of lace. If needed, lay a piece of silicone paper over the top and give a firm rub to secure the lace (a). Continue to add lace, leaving the outline that will be visible in a free-form organic shape. It can help to tear the lace rather than cut it to get a more natural look.

2. Next apply the metallic leafing. This is done in a similar way to applying the fishnet (see also Metallic Techniques: Leafing). Wet the surface again with a paintbrush dipped in water and blot with tissue. Start with the silver leaf and apply to the area closest to where the larger beaded flower will sit. Don't press down the entire sheet, just enough to make a large patch of silver (b).

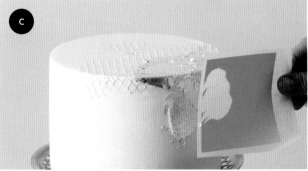

3. Now move on to the lemon gold leaf (c). Continue to wet areas, blot them with tissue and apply the transfer sheets, moving on to the green gold and then the gold. The leafing can extend outside the line of the fishnet. It adds complexity to overlay a few flecks of contrasting colour, for example adding a few flecks of silver leaf over the yellow gold areas. Wet and blot before adding the flecks.

4. Roll out the white fondant to around 1mm (1/32in) thick and cut around 45 small four-petal blossoms (d). These can be used to make sugar blossoms, but applied flat to the side of the cake they look like stylised crosses. It's helpful to keep them covered while working as they can dry out quickly.

5. Apply the blossom 'crosses' to the side of the cake, starting with a diagonal line of around six crosses. Use piping gel brushed on to the back of the crosses to adhere them to the cake. Add a couple more rows, offsetting the positioning so that the edge becomes a little free-form rather than blocky. When a small area is done, use an embosser to impress a pattern into the appliqué (e). My embosser is a square cut from a plastic tablecloth, but any lace or pattern embosser will work. Continue to add crosses and emboss them until the area to the right of centre at the front of the cake is covered roughly in a slightly random way.

6. Cut about 50 tiny leaf shapes from gumpaste rolled to less than 1mm (1/32in) thick. Use a balling tool on a petal pad to thin them out and create a cupped shape (f). It can be helpful to keep the gumpaste pieces covered both while working on the balling and after they are shaped. It will be easier to adhere them to the cake if they are not too dried out.

7. Apply the leaf shapes so that they create a curved line across the front of the cake, starting at the top edge to the right and sweeping down to the left (g). Adhere the leaves using piping gel and press firmly to secure them. Add more leaves above and below, creating a strong line that has some organic and random finishing.

8. Fold some wafer paper into about four. You can also use offcuts for this if you have them. Make wafer 'sequins' by using a 6mm (1/4in) hole punch to cut out the tiny circles (h). It will be faster if you can cut through more than one layer of wafer at a time, hence folding the paper into four.

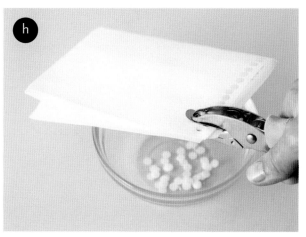

9. Put the circles into a bowl and add a little white lustre powder. Swirl with a brush until the circles have a pearlised sheen (i).

10. Apply two or three rows of sequins above the feathered leaves. Pipe a small 2.5–5cm (1–2in) line of royal icing using a no.2 piping nozzle (tip), and then place the sequins. The support of the royal icing allows you to place the sequins on a slight angle away from the surface of the cake making a more natural and dimensional look. Use a small paintbrush dipped in piping gel to pick up and transfer the sequins onto the cake (j). If needed, tweak the positioning or angle of the sequins with a cocktail stick (toothpick) or needle tool.

11. Take a small piece of fondant and dip it in water, then knead the water through so the fondant is very tacky. The ball should be only 2cm (¾in) or less in diameter. Place it on the cake where the line of feathered leaves starts (k).

12. Push carrot-shaped dragees into the ball around the base (l). If your ball is the right size, it should take about 12 silver dragees. Next add a layer of approximately nine pear-shaped dragees. Push them in on an angle above the layer of carrots. Make the innermost layer with seed shapes and finish in the centre with a single button shape. On the side of the cake below the big flower, create a second smaller flower. The fondant ball for this one should be only 1cm (about ½in) in diameter. All the petals on this flower are seed-shaped dragees. The base layer should take about 12 seeds and the inner row about nine seeds on an angle. The centre is a single 8mm (⅜in) silver ball.

13. Using the rice-shaped dragees, create two curved lines down the side of the cake starting at the larger flower. To stick these on, paint a fine line of piping gel and then use tweezers to place the beads (m). Press in with your fingers if needed but be careful not to handle them too much as the silver can come off. At every second rice bead, add two more rice beads on an angle to resemble leaves. The finished beading will look like vines. Add a few more short lines or 'tendrils' if it looks good and is balanced.

14. Add some 10mm (½in) and 5mm (¼in) edible pearls by painting a dab of piping gel and then pushing them in firmly. The concentration of beads should be heavier around the focal point of the flower. Don't make them too evenly scattered; it's better if there are a few small groups and some areas left open (n).

SUGAR COOKIES

A pretty co-ordinating treat to go with this cake would be a super sweet stack of sugar cookies, sandwiched with piped white chocolate ganache. Top with crisp white fondant and decorate with a single silver bead flower and a small sweep of feathered leaves.

Molten Drizzle

Outgoing yet poised, this molten gold drizzle cake uses punchy hot pink washes and plenty of gold. The elements of this cake look technical but are readily achievable. The ombre pink watercolour effect is painted on to the stacked tiers, and both the truffles and the gilded wafer paper should be prepared the day before assembling the cake for ease of handling.

Materials

- Two round white fondant-covered cake tiers, dowelled and stacked, in the following sizes: 10cm (4in) diameter by 12.5cm (5in) tall and 12.5cm (5in) diameter by 15cm (6in) tall

- Isomalt, 250g (9oz)

- Pegs

- Edible pen

- Extra fondant to support sails

- Tapered palette knife or paring knife

- Petal dusts, light pink and hot pink

- Cake decorator's alcohol (95%)

- Fine paintbrush

- Royal icing, 200g (7oz)

- Piping nozzle (tip), no.4 round, plus piping bag

- Edible lustre powders (Faye Cahill Cake Design Lustre), Regency Gold, Merlot, Ivory Champagne, Rose Quartz and Mocha

- Hard white chocolate ganache, 150g (5½oz)

- Cocktail sticks (toothpicks)

- Candy Melts or compound white chocolate

- Wafer paper, one sheet

- Piping gel

- Gold leaf, 23- or 24-carat, two transfer sheets

- 6mm (¼in) hole punch

1. The glassy sails on this cake are made from isomalt, which is a diet sugar. It's a little technical to use but you can get the hang of it really fast and it's lots of fun to play with. Use a lot of caution while working with molten sugar as any burns could be severe. Have some iced water on hand just in case! Prepare the isomalt (see Tip), then pour a little out onto a silicone work mat. I used the back of my fishnet lace mat and the very faint fishnet impression was a subtle and interesting texture. Tilt the mat to spread the isomalt (a). It cools very fast so work quickly while being careful not to touch the sugar. You are aiming for a roughly rectangular shape with the isomalt evenly spread. If you find you have a thicker section, try to put that at the base of the sail and leave the top looking nice and light.

Isomalt can be purchased in either brick or nib form. The bricks simply need to be heated till liquid. The nibs are put in a pan with just a couple of tablespoons of water and heated to 165–180°C (325–350°F). Use a candy thermometer to check the temperature. The isomalt should not be stirred during heating, but you can lift and swirl the pan to incorporate any unmelted nibs.

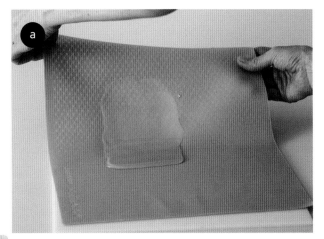

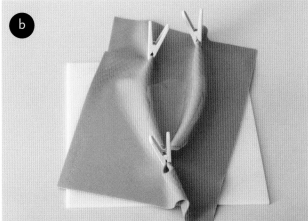

2. When the shape is looking good, use pegs to create folds in the sail (b). The aim is to make the bottom gather in more and the top to flare out with gentle folds. Make two sails for this cake, one smaller and one larger, with heights between 10cm and 15cm (4in and 6in) and widths of 7.5cm to 12.5cm (3in to 5in).

3. Dig a hole at the back of the top tier with a sharp knife. To estimate the shape of the hole, hold the sail in position and use an edible marker to create an outline, then repeat for the second sail. The holes should be roughly 2.5–4cm (1–1½in) deep. Position the first sail and then use some kneaded fondant to fill around the sail and support it. Position the second smaller sail and support that with fondant too (c).

4. Level and smooth off any excess fondant to make it flush with the cake surface. A paring knife or tapered palette knife is good for this process (d).

5. The gold drips are created with plain white royal icing that has been thinned with water. Add just a little water at a time when mixing the royal icing. The consistency can be tested before applying it to the real cake: use a vertical surface such as a cake tin or foam dummy and pipe some drips, giving them plenty of time to run out fully. Be patient. It's very easy to make the icing too thin so that the drips run all the way to the base of the cake instead of having a nice variation of lengths. When ready to apply drips to the cake, start at the top edge of the top tier and pipe out some royal icing, allowing it to drizzle down the side (e). Pipe out more for longer drips and less for shorter. Try to make the drips a bit irregular in their lengths and spacing for a more natural look.

6. When drips on the sides are done, pipe out some more royal icing onto the top surface of the cake and use a palette knife to spread it. Work it all the way up to the base of the sails for a seamless look (f). Repeat the drip making process on the bottom tier. I like the look of longer drips on the bottom tier and shorter on the top. Allow everything to set for at least half an hour before painting the drips gold.

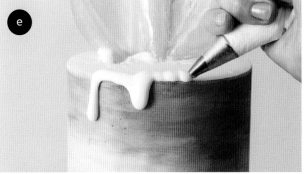

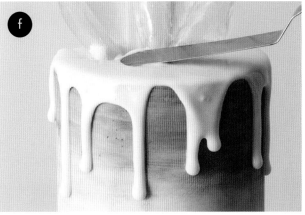

7. The confetti dots for the sails are made with gilded wafer paper (see Metallic Techniques: Leafing, Gilding Wafer Paper). Since the sails are clear, it's nice to gild both sides of the wafer paper. One sheet of gold leaf on either side of a piece of wafer paper should be enough to make about 100 dots, sufficient for this cake. Prepare the gilded paper at least a day in advance so the paper is not sticky from freshly applied gel. Don't use the spray glaze for this one either as it has a tackiness that can also cause the dots to stick together. Punch out the dots one at a time rather than doubling over the paper (g). Spread them out on a flat surface so they don't stick together.

8. Use a fine paintbrush dipped in piping gel to pick the confetti dots up and apply them to the sail (h). Spread them in a random pattern, not too evenly spaced. Some can overlap a little and some areas can be left more open. Create a 'cascading' look that's heavier at the top and graduates down to clear sails at the base.

9. Highlight the top edge of the sails with a strong gold lustre such as Regency Gold (i). Mix lustre powder with the cake decorator's alcohol to a smooth consistency and paint it on with a fine brush. Extend the highlighting down the sides of the sails, tapering off towards the base.

10. When the royal icing is firm enough, continue with the same gold paint and highlight all of the drips and the top surfaces of the cake tiers (j). Use a fine paintbrush to get right in on the sides of the drips. A larger one can be used over the bigger areas at the top.

11. The truffles are made from white chocolate ganache that has been rolled into balls and dipped in white chocolate. Use a firmer mix of ganache, the same as you would use for masking a cake (see Recipes, and General Techniques: Assembling). With the ganache solid at room temperature, pinch or cut off a little piece and quickly roll it around in your hands to form a ball (k). You don't get much working time with these as they will soften up quickly with the heat of your hand. If needed, put the ball into the fridge to cool and then roll again to get a more perfect shape. Insert a cocktail stick (toothpick) into the truffle and refrigerate until cool.

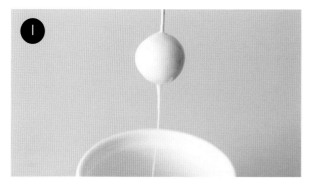

12. Melt some white Candy Melts or white chocolate buttons. Since these are more of a decorative feature, you can use a compound white chocolate that will not need to be tempered. Microwave the chocolate or melts for 10–20 seconds at a time and stir until liquid. Dip the cooled truffles into the melted chocolate and hold over the bowl to allow the excess to flow off (l). I like to hold them there for quite a while to allow the coating to begin to set. That way, when I turn a truffle the right way up, I can get a nice little trail across the top of the ball, which adds a cool detail. Leave them upright to dry by inserting the cocktail stick (toothpick) into a piece of styrofoam. These should be prepared in advance and left overnight to set.

13. The truffles are coloured with a dry brush technique (m). The fat content of the chocolate will make the lustre powder adhere to the ball. For the stronger colours, you can use a painting technique by mixing the powder with cake decorator's alcohol if the colour is not strong enough with the dry brushing. On this cake I have used Ivory Champagne, Merlot, Mocha and two mid pinks made by mixing some pink petal dusts into the Rose Quartz colour.

14. Use tweezers to grip the cocktail sticks (toothpicks) and insert the truffles into the cake (n). Create a tapered cascade with some truffles sitting higher than others for a full and rounded look. I added a single truffle on the lower tier to give visual interest.

PETITE CAKE

Reverse out the colours to make this precious mini. The petite cake is gilded with 23-carat gold leaf and the royal icing is tinted hot pink before drizzling. Dress it up with a single truffle and some arty isomalt!

Glam Rock Trio

A trio of rockstar cakes that will be a solid gold hit at any party! In fact these luxe beauties use a fair amount of solid golds and silvers, so don't forget to factor in the material costs of the edible metallic leafs. The decorating process for these is not too difficult once the leafing process is mastered. A combination of sharp geometric elements and artful torn edges makes this group really rock.

Materials

- Octagon cake – two dark-grey fondant-covered cake tiers, in the following sizes: 12.5cm (5in) diameter round, 8cm (3¼in) tall, and 15cm (6in) diameter octagon, 15cm (6in) tall. Note: the diameter is measured from flat edge to flat edge.

- Cylinder cake – one white fondant-covered cylinder, 12.5cm (5in) diameter, 14cm (5½in) tall

- Cube cake – one white fondant-covered cube, 10cm (4in) x 10cm (4in) x 10cm (4in)

- Silver leaf, one book of 25 transfer sheets

- Gold leaf, 23- or 24-carat, one book of 25 transfer sheets

- Lemon gold leaf (16-carat), 10 transfer sheets

- White gold leaf (12-carat), two transfer sheets

- Green gold leaf (18-carat), two transfer sheets

- Wafer paper, four sheets

- Edible spray glaze

- 2mm (1⁄16in) silver dragees, 100g (3½oz)

- Piping gel

- Fresh or dried blooms and foliage such as leucadendron, sea holly or thistle

- Florist's tape

- Cake decorator's alcohol (95%)

- Edible lustre powder (Faye Cahill Cake Design Lustre), Regency Gold

1. Get started by applying the gold and silver leaf (see Metallic Techniques: Leafing) to all the cakes. The cube has all surfaces covered in silver, except the bottom third of the sides, which can be left without silver leaf as they will be covered by the gold wafer paper later. The cylinder has the sides covered gold and the top surface in silver. For the octagon cake, cover the top surface of the bottom tier in gold leaf (you only need to cover the area that will show after the top tier is stacked), then you can stack on the top tier and cover the top surface of that tier in silver leaf. Finally, gild two sheets of wafer paper in gold (using six transfer sheets per piece of wafer paper), and one and a half wafer paper sheets each of silver and lemon gold leaf.

2. For the cylinder cake, pour the tiny silver dragees into a tray that is big enough to lay the cylinder on its side in. Add a fresh spray of edible glaze to the sides of the cylinder cake. Be very liberal with the spray; the purpose of the glaze is to make the sides sticky so the dragees will adhere to it. Immediately transfer the cake to the tray and roll it so the sprinkles stick to the sides (a). Work quickly to add the sprinkles before the glaze dries.

3. After rolling, carefully set the cake upright and look for any empty areas. More dragees can be added by scooping up a handful from the tray and applying them directly to the cake (b). Remove the cake from the tray and the cylinder cake is now finished. The reflective gold combined with the tiny shiny silver balls creates a really cool optical effect, and nothing more is needed to make it shine.

All of the leafing is better done the day before decorating to allow it to set, and the wafer sheets should be sprayed with edible glaze after leafing to allow for better handling. The leafed parts of the cakes will also benefit from a spray of glaze after leafing so they handle better while decorating.

4. For the cube cake, take one of the sheets of gilded wafer paper and cut a strip that is 7.5cm (3in) wide and long enough to wrap around two sides of the cube (c).

5. Use a ruler to create a sharp fold in the centre, then place the wafer paper against the cube cake and mark exactly where the cake edge finishes. Trim the strip so that the cut edges will fit the sides of the cube exactly, then create a tear on an angle across the top of the strip as shown (d).

6. Lay the piece of wafer with the gold side down and paint the back completely with piping gel. Keep the torn section that will not be used on the cube, as it can be used on the octagon cake. Apply the wafer paper to the cube, pressing firmly so it adheres well (e). To avoid damage while handling, a sheet of silicone paper can be used to protect the cake and wafer paper while applying pressure. Now two of the sides are covered, the process can be repeated for the other two sides. When making the tear across the edge, measure it against the one already applied so the tear looks continuous over all four faces. This completes the cube cake.

7. For the octagon cake, begin by creating an ombre gradient of metallic leafs on the top tier of the two tier cake. The tier is 8cm (3¼in) tall and you have five colours to apply, so each stripe will be around 1.6cm (⅝in). Start by cutting the sheets of leaf into strips of around this size. The strips should look neat but very slightly irregular, so there's no need to measure them exactly. Cut them by hand with scissors rather than using a ruler and blade (f).

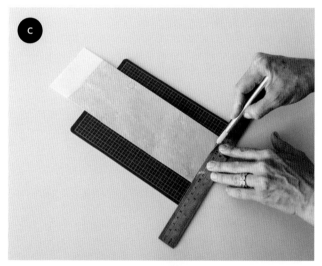

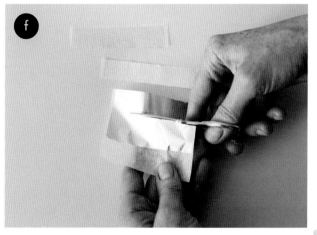

8. Apply the cut pieces one at a time (the technique is described fully in Metallic Techniques: Leafing), starting with the top row of silver and working down through each colour (g). The sequence starts with the silver leaf at the top, the second stripe is white gold, then lemon gold, green gold and finishes at the bottom with the 23- or 24-carat gold. Check the stickiness of each section of fondant before applying the strip. After the last strip is added, if the bottom edge looks a little ragged, run a dry paintbrush around the edge to smooth out the leaf and remove any loose bits.

9. The process of applying the torn wafer paper to the octagon cake is a bit like pâpier maché or decoupage. You need some of the wafer paper pieces to have straight edges and right angles so the panels are defined nicely, so start by trimming the wafer paper down using a ruler and blade. After creating the straight edges, the sheets can be torn into irregular size pieces (h). Start by tearing up around three quarters of a sheet of each silver, lemon gold and 23- or 24-carat gold. Leave the rest intact so that there is extra to create more straight edges or particular size pieces as needed when creating the pattern.

10. Start by applying the pieces that have straight edges, and line them up with the edges of the octagon panels. Paint the back of each piece of gilded wafer paper with piping gel before applying it to the cake (i).

11. Fill out the middle of each panel with the fully torn pieces, tucking them under other pieces where needed until the panel resembles a nice strong piece of marble. Rub firmly over the panel using silicone paper as a barrier so your fingers don't get sticky (j). Make sure all pieces are firmly adhered.

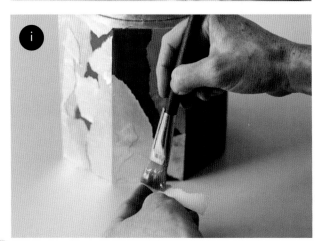

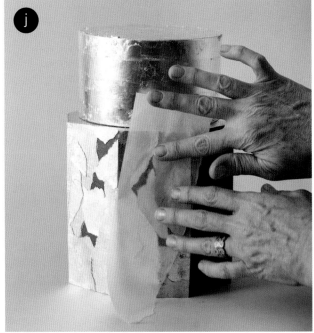

12. The floral feature is created using an arrangement of natural blooms and foliage. I used a dried leucadendron and some fresh native leaves, but you can select anything you wish. The flower is highlighted with a paint made from gold edible lustre mixed with cake decorator's alcohol. Only highlight the tips of the brushy centre in gold, but paint the surrounding petals fully (k).

13. Paint the green leaves roughly in a washy gold, using the same paint. Then use florist's tape to bind the ends of the natural blooms and foliage making them safe to insert into the cake (l). Fully bind any section of stem that will be in contact with the cake.

14. Finally, add the floral feature to the cake (m). Long-nose pliers can help when arranging the flowers. I like my blooms to sit nice and tight against the cake surface and the pliers make it easier than using hands, especially where it's necessary to grip the bloom very close to the flower head.

THE GILDED TRUFFLE

Individual chocolate mousse desserts, glazed in shiny dark chocolate ganache, can be decorated with gilded wafer paper, artfully torn into arcs to create a stylish crown.

Chocolate & Gold Splash

A match made in heaven, chocolate and gold is a classic combination, given a twist here by the application of metallic leaf and splatters. Copper tinted spheres add to the contemporary look with fresh flowers complementing the rich palette. Remember to glaze the cake and make the chocolate spheres the day before decorating.

Materials

- Three round chocolate fondant-covered cake tiers, dowelled and stacked in the following sizes: 10cm (4in) diameter by 10cm (4in) tall, 12.5cm (5in) diameter by 10cm (4in) tall, and 15cm (6in) diameter by 12.5cm (5in) tall

- Coverture dark chocolate, 100g (3½oz)

- Candy thermometer

- Cotton gloves

- Gold leaf, 23- or 24-carat, 15 transfer sheets

- Silicone paper, 36 x 36cm (14 x 14in)

- Edible glaze

- Plastic florist's tape (Parafilm), green

- Florist's wire, 24-gauge green, two or three pieces

- Edible lustre powders (Faye Cahill Cake Design Lustre), Regency Gold and Copper

- Cake decorator's alcohol (95%)

- Stiff pastry brush

1. You can use compound chocolate to make the spheres and if you do, tempering is not required: just melt in a microwave in 20-second bursts, checking and stirring after each interval until the chocolate has no lumps and is fully melted. However, using coverture chocolate will result in glossier spheres that are also more delicious. Melt two thirds of the chocolate in a microwave, checking and stirring every 20 seconds. The chocolate should be fluid and smooth, and between 50 and 55°C (122 and 131°F) (a). Add the remaining third of the chocolate and stir briskly to cool the mixture and start the process of encouraging the crystals to align. The chocolate will be tempered when the temperature drops to 31–32°C (88–89.5°F).

2. Remove any unmelted chunks at this point and then pour the chocolate into moulds. Pour at least four 4cm (1½in) diameter half-spheres and another four of the smaller 2.5cm (1in) diameter ones. Extras are always good to have on hand as they are easily damaged during handling. Scrape over the top of the mould with a palette knife to level the filled hollows (b).

3. Refrigerate or leave the chocolate overnight until set and then unmould the solid hemispheres (c).

4. Use cotton gloves to avoid marking the chocolate with your fingers. Heat a metal item such as a pan or scraper on a hotplate until warm. Press the flat side of one hemisphere onto the heated metal until it melts slightly (d).

5. Quickly attach it to another hemisphere to form a full sphere (e). Hold the chocolate pieces in place until the melted surface sets and the two sides stay together. After creating all the spheres, colour them with a paint made from Copper lustre and cake decorator's alcohol, using the same method as for the truffles on the Molten Drizzle cake (see Molten Drizzle, step 13).

6. Glaze the cake with edible glaze. Leave overnight for the glaze to dry before decorating, then cover the entire top tier and top surface of the second tier in gold leaf (see Metallic Techniques: Leafing). The edible glaze may still be slightly sticky after drying, in which case the leaf will stick easily without any extra application of water. On the sides of the second tier, cover the upper section of the cake in gold leaf, leaving an uneven edge. It will help to use offcuts and remainders of gold leaf transfer sheets that already have an irregular edge (f).

7. Cut a 12.5cm (5in) circle from the centre of a piece of silicone paper about 36 x 36cm (14 x 14in) in size. Make a cut to the back and wrap around the base of the second tier to mask off the bottom tier so it doesn't get too many splatters on it (g).

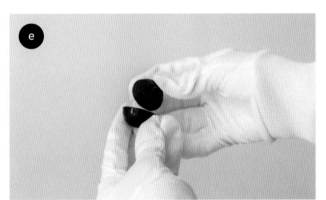

8. Mix an edible gold paint using Regency Gold lustre and alcohol. Use a stiff pastry brush or new toothbrush to flick splatters of gold paint onto the cake, creating a graduation of heavier coverage near the leafing and lighter towards the base of tier. You want a mixture of large and small splatters and the stiff brush will help to achieve these. Another tip is to use a thicker mixture of lustre, around 50:50 ratio of lustre to alcohol (h).

9. Take a pea-sized ball of fondant and dip it in water. Knead it until tacky and then place it on the top tier, near the front and offset to the left side (i).

10. Press one of the larger size spheres into the fondant ball to secure it (j). Check carefully to make sure the fondant is not visible at the front and then repeat the process to add a smaller sphere to the side of the larger one. Add a large and small sphere at the base of the cake using the same method to secure, offsetting these ones to the right side.

11. To prepare fresh flowers to decorate the cake, the stems need to be well sealed with florist's tape, and wires added to strengthen the stems. Use a length of 24-gauge green florist's wire to pierce through the base of the flower (k).

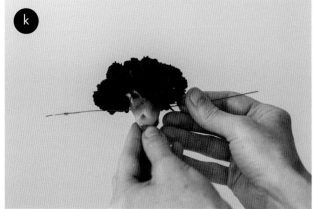

12. For a pierced or hooked stem, bend the two ends of the wire so they are in line with the stem and use plastic florist's tape (Parafilm) to bind them together (l).

13. The flowers can be secured by sticking a ball of fondant to the top of the cake and pushing the wires into the fondant. If the stems are to go into the cake, they need to be made food safe by using a wax seal or covering the wire with a food safe product like a drinking straw. Offset the blooms to the right of the spheres and trail some filler or foliage down the side of the cake for a modern look (m).

If the fresh flowers for the cake need to be on display for any length of time, add in a small pinch of wet kitchen paper at the base of the stem to keep the flower from wilting too quickly. Of course, bind in the wet paper very carefully so it is fully sealed.

SEVEN SINS

Indulge in a rich double-chocolate cake layered with dark ganache and topped with a milk chocolate swirl, a coppered truffle, an edible rose petal and splash of gold.

Treasured Laurel Lace

Crisp white and brilliant gold are paired with delicate lace details on this sweet two tier cake. Decorated with fine stencilled lace and embellished with appliqué, piping and feathery gumpaste textures, the Treasured Laurel Lace cake celebrates cherished love.

Materials

- Two round white fondant-covered cakes tiers, in the following sizes: 10cm (4in) diameter by 10cm (4in) tall, and 15cm (6in) diameter by 12.5cm (5in) tall

- Gold leaf, 23- or 24-carat, 16 transfer sheets

- Lace stencil, Faye Cahill Cake Design, Mandala Lace stencil

- Royal icing, 100g (3½oz)

- Piping nozzle (tip), no.1, plus piping bag

- Paintbrush

- Gumpaste, 100g (3½oz)

- Florist's wire, 24-gauge, five pieces

- Long-nose pliers

- Dogwood flower cutters, 6cm (2⅜in) and 4.5cm (1¾in)

- Frilly/fancy leaf cutter, 5cm (2in)

- Sugar glue

- Balling tool and petal pad

1. The feathery ruffles of gumpaste should be made the day prior to decorating, or set in a dehydrator. For this cake you need gumpaste pieces for both the ruffles and appliqué. The wired ruffles are made from sections cut with the large dogwood flower cutter (6cm (2⅜in) diameter) and the frilly/fancy leaf which is around 5cm (2in) long. Any similar frilled or fluted shaped cutter will be fine. All pieces should be cut from thin gumpaste 1–2mm (about 1/16in) thick. Cut the leaves in half lengthwise, and then roll them by hand to thin and extend them. Transfer the pieces onto a petal pad and use a balling tool to shape and cup the frilled edges (a).

2. Cut the lengths of 24-gauge florist's wire into quarters, then form hooks by bending several at a time with long-nose pliers (b). Clamp from the other side with pliers to close the hook fully.

3. Paint a line of sugar glue along the straight edge of the gumpaste piece. Scrunch some folds into the base and insert the hook into one of the folds (c).

4. Pinch and refine the base of the piece with your fingers to shape it into a neat taper (d). Hang it upside down to dry. Make around eight of this style of ruffle.

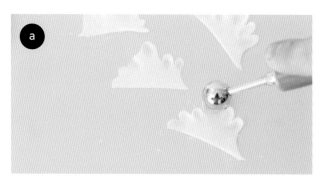

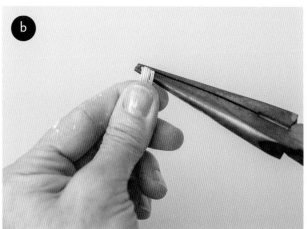

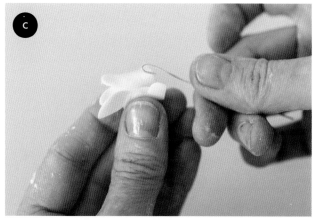

5. The smaller ruffles are made by dividing off individual petals of the large dogwood shape, as shown (e).

6. Roll out each petal to thin and extend it, then shape and frill with the balling tool (f). Scrunch the base and add sugar glue, then a hooked wire. Press and neaten the base as before. Hang upside down to dry. Make around 12 of the smaller ruffles.

7. Before decorating the cakes, cover the entire bottom tier in gold leaf (see Metallic Techniques: Leafing), including the part of the top surface that will not be covered by the top tier. Spray with edible glaze and allow to dry. Stack the top tier (see General Techniques: Dowelling & Stacking) and apply gold leaf to a section of that tier, offset to the side. Make a template for the fine dots by drawing a 1cm (½in) grid on paper. Make a mark on every second junction along the first row, then offset the dot on the row below marking every second point. Continue for all rows. Pin the template to the cake, securing it at points that have dots, and then use a large pin to mark out dots over the entire two tiers of cake (g). At the back there will be a section where the template joins and dots will not match up exactly. Just leave a 2–3cm (¾–1¼in) gap here and freehand in the dots later as they may need different spacing.

8. Royal icing for stencilling needs to be a reasonably stiff mix. If it's too soft you are more likely to get bleeding and imperfections. For good coverage of white over gold, add some white gel or paste colour. It will be brighter and more opaque, and will make a nice clear contrast against the gold. Pin the stencil to the top tier, inserting the pins at points where they will be covered. Spread the royal icing thinly over the area that has been covered in gold (h). The stencil can go outside the gold line a little. Don't make it too neat.

9. Scrape back the royal icing using firm strokes and a couple of passes of the scraper (i). Remove pins and do an additional scrape over those points to fill the pin holes: a smaller palette knife is better for this (see Metallic Techniques: Leafing, Stencilling Over Leaf).

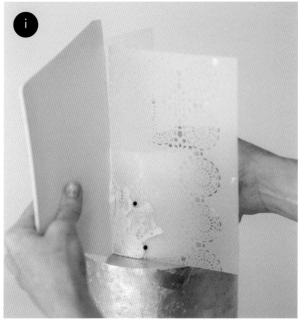

10. Wash and thoroughly dry the stencil, then pin it over the bottom tier. For this tier, it's good to mask off the stencil at the height of the tier to prevent any excess royal icing bleeding onto the top surface of the tier. Spread the royal icing over the stencil, starting by making a rough line that follows the line of the gold section above (j). Fill out the area to the left of that line and continue to fill around half of the cake, finishing with a similar diagonal line.

11. Scrape back the royal icing as before, and then peel off the stencil to reveal the lace pattern on the bottom tier (k).

12. Pipe fine dots of royal icing over all of the marked points that are not covered by the stencil. To pipe a dot, place the piping nozzle (tip) as close as possible to the surface of the cake without touching it. Squeeze out a small dot of icing, stop squeezing and then pull the nozzle away (l). Pipe out a few dots at a time and then go back with a damp paintbrush and pat down the peaks of the dots so they have a rounded shape.

13. Now add the gumpaste ruffles that you made in steps 1–6. They can be applied to the top tier to form a natural curve that extends a little past the top edge of the tier and sweeps down the side. Coat the wires to make them food safe if needed before inserting into the cake (see Chocolate & Gold Splash, steps 11–13). Leave a small section without wired ruffles towards the base of the tier (m).

14. Take a single gumpaste flower cut with the 4.5cm (1¾in) cutter and roll to extend. Try to roll one side more than the other so the final flower is no longer symmetrical – it creates a more natural look. Use sugar glue to attach this piece to the bottom tier on the edge of the stencil. Press to secure (n).

15. Make some smaller ruffle pieces from this size flower cutter using the same method as described in steps 1–6, except without the wire. Use sugar glue or royal icing to secure these to the cake above and below the single flower, including on to the top tier (o).

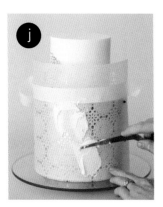

16. Add detail to the main flower by piping tapered lines on the petals using the same no.1 piping nozzle (tip) (p). Then add some dots in the centre.

17. Pipe several daisy-style flowers using long teardrop shaped strokes (q). Pipe a dot in the centre to finish.

18. Add some trailing leaf details by piping a line that extends from the floral section, and then add leaves using a 'stitched' zig zag line, as shown (r). This is created by skimming the piping tip back and forth across the surface of the cake while squeezing out a line of icing. The beauty of a freehand style lace like this is that you can add extra motifs if needed to cover imperfections or fill out the design. Check for balance in your design, and adjust if needed.

TREASURED RINGS

Mini cakes baked in the shape of donuts can be decorated with sparkling sanding sugar, edible pearls, gold leaf and sugar flowers. The pure white icing invites the tastebuds to sample its delicate flavour.

Fall Foliage

This foliage topped cake is for those who like their glam understated. Choosing leaves and a few fruits over popular blooms is the choice of someone confident with their personal style, who likes to do things a little left of centre. The metallic treatment of the crabapples and foliage brings to mind treasured keepsakes and heirloom jewellery.

Materials

- Three round soft blue fondant-covered cake tiers, dowelled and stacked, in the following sizes: 10cm (4in), 18cm (7in) and 25cm (10in) diameter, each one 7.5cm (3in) tall

- Airbrush and compressor

- Edible lustre powders (Faye Cahill Cake Design Lustre), Copper, Bronze, Signature Gold, Regency Gold, Graphite, Rich Coco and Flash Silver

- Cake decorator's alcohol (95%)

- Foam balls, 2cm (¾in) and 1.5cm (⅝in)

- Florist's wire, 18-, 22-, 24- and 28-gauge

- Wire cutters and long-nose pliers

- Hot glue gun

- Florist's tape, white and green

- Gumpaste, approx 200g (7oz)

- Cutters: 3.5cm (1⅜in) rose leaf, 3cm (1⅛in), 4cm (1½in) and 5.5cm (2¼in) leaf, 7cm (2¾in) fern, 3cm (1⅛in) and 5cm (2in) water lily petals

- Modelling tools, frilling tool, Dresden tool and balling tool

- Petal pad

- Bumpy foam pad

- Double-sided general leaf veiner

- Magnolia leaf veiner

- Gardenia leaf veiner

- Edible paint or airbrush colour, green and brown

- Edible glaze spray

- Green-tinted modelling chocolate, 100g (3½oz)

- Peach and ivory fondant, 50g (1¾oz) of each

- Piping gel or sugar glue

- Fine scissors

- Medium double-headed stamens

- Royal icing

- Piping nozzle (tip), 1.5 writing, plus piping bag

1. To make the crabapples, start by attaching foam balls to sections of 18-gauge wire with a hot glue gun. Pierce a hole in the ball using the wire, then add glue to the wire and re-insert it into the hole (a). More of the glue will get into the hole that way and will give the bond the strength it needs to hold the weight of the finished crabapple. Make three 2cm (¾in) diameter centres and two 1.5cm (⅝in).

2. Wrap the wire in green florist's tape (b), then paint the foam ball lightly with piping gel or sugar glue so the paste will adhere to it. Mix a little fondant and green-tinted modelling chocolate, then soften the colour by also adding some peach and ivory fondant. This mix will blend together nicely and the seams will be easy to smooth out. Wrap a layer of this kneaded paste over the foam ball.

3. Cut off the excess paste at the base of the ball, then roll the ball in your hands until it forms a smooth shape and there are no seams and cracks visible. Use a balling tool to indent the top of the crabapple, creating a small rounded hollow. Create grooves that run away from the top indentation using a modelling tool such as a frilling tool (c). Make these a little irregular and running only a little way down the side of the apple. Soften both the grooves and the top indentation with your fingers to integrate them.

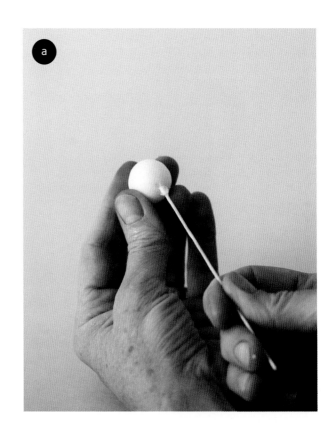

4. Attach a very small ball of paste into the indentation, using piping gel to adhere it to the crabapple. Snip into the little ball with fine scissors to create tiny spikes that resemble the core-end of the crabapple (d). Repeat this process for all five apples – there will be three larger and two smaller ones – then set them aside to let the paste firm up overnight. If the arrangement is put together while the paste is still soft, flat patches will form where the crabapples touch each other.

5. Tape the five finished crabapples together with green florist's tape (e). You may need to bend the stems a little to make them sit nicely.

6. Roll out some gumpaste to 1.5mm (⅝in) thickness. Cut nine leaves using a 3.5cm (1⅜in) long leaf cutter with a fluted edge, such as a rose leaf cutter, then cut a full length of 24-gauge wire into four even pieces and insert one halfway into each leaf (f).

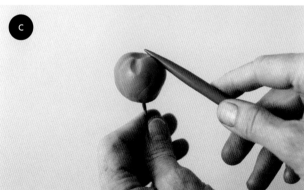

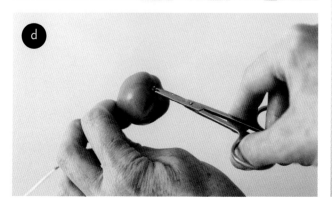

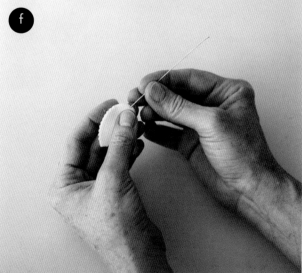

7. Roll out the leaf to extend and thin the edges. Ideally you want to end up with finished leaves varying in size a little from about 4–5cm (1½–2in). Use a general leaf veiner to emboss the veins onto the leaf. Line up the leaf with centre vein and down press firmly (g).

8. On a petal pad, run a balling tool firmly around the edge of the leaf, creating soft curls in the edge (h).

9. With the leaf still on a petal pad, use a Dresden tool to score a groove down the centre of the leaf, which will cause the sides to angle up in a natural 'v' shape. Lay the leaves to dry in bumpy foam, allowing the bumps to support the curls in the edges (i). Once dry, wrap the wires in green florist's tape to match the crabapples.

10. Paint each leaf with an alcohol wash tinted with a drop each of green and brown edible paint or airbrush colour, using a soft brush, then tape the leaves together in groups of two and three with green florist's tape (j).

11. Add the leaf sprigs around the crabapple bunch. Attaching them with florist's tape and making the front stem longer so the leaves trail down (k).

12. Highlight the apples and leaves with copper edible lustre mixed with alcohol (l). Concentrate the stronger colour on one side of the apple only, using a 'watered down' mix (thinned with more alcohol) to lighten the colour over other areas. Leave some unpainted green showing. On the leaves, highlight all edges and paint some leaves solid copper on one side of the centre groove. Use the thinner mix to paint over other areas. Some green will show through the areas that have been painted more thinly. Paint all the leaf backs in copper, then spray the arrangement with edible glaze to set the lustre.

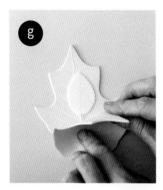

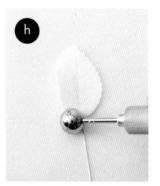

13. The stem at the front of the arrangement is seeded eucalyptus. The seeds are a really cool feature to add interest to a foliage arrangement. Start by cutting a medium double-headed stamen in half, then take a tiny pinch of gumpaste and wrap it around the stamen head (m). If the gumpaste is a little sticky, you may not need to use sugar glue.

14. Roll the paste between your fingers to make a tapered shape at the bottom. Pinch off any excess if needed. The top will form into a ball above your fingers from the rolling motion. The finished seed should measure around 1cm (½in). Then pinch the upper side of the seed head so it forms a gentle peak (n).

15. Tape together seven seeds to make one seed head, using white florist's tape. The eucalyptus branch has three seed heads, so we will need 21 individual seeds Add in a length of 24-gauge wire for structure. Leave one seed pointing upright and bend the other six so they sit at a right angle to the stem and form a star shape (o).

16. Next tape the three seed heads together at different heights (p), then add five simple leaves. To make the leaves use a 3cm (1⅛in) general leaf cutter and a general leaf veiner. Cut the five leaves, insert a 24-gauge wire into each one, then roll them out to extend and thin the leaf – the finished size should be around 3.5cm (1⅜in). These should be dried reasonably flat, they don't have much shape. Tape the leaves at the base of the eucalyptus stem with white florist's tape, placing them at different heights.

17. Paint the stem and leaves in a neutral gold lustre such as Signature Gold, and the seed heads a charcoal lustre such as Graphite Black (q). Blend the two colours together on the stem near the seed heads. Spray with edible glaze to set the lustre.

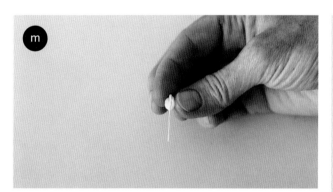

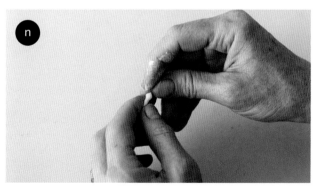

18. Next create the fern. It has a very detailed shape and so it can be hard to remove the gumpaste from the cutter. Roll the gumpaste to about 1.5mm (⅝in) thick, and press the fern cutter into it. To make sure the gumpaste is completely cut in all areas, turn the cutter over and use a small rolling pin to rub over and expose the cutter through the gumpaste. Pull away the excess gumpaste (r), using a skewer or needle tool to remove any tiny pieces that remain, then push the fern piece out of the cutter from behind.

19. Trim the fern stem down to make it easier to thread in the wire and get it further into the fern leaf. Thread a length of 24-gauge wire as far into the fern as possible. Try to get it almost to the end. On a petal pad, thin and slightly shape the fern with a balling tool (s).

20. Vein the fern by pressing between a double-sided general leaf veiner (t). Lay on bumpy foam to dry, arranging the extended parts of the leaves so they look a bit irregular and natural.

21. The finished leaf will have a point where the wire goes into the leaf that needs filling out with florist's tape to make the transition nicer. Wrap multiple layers of white tape around the wire until the thickness of the wire matches the gumpaste stem (u).

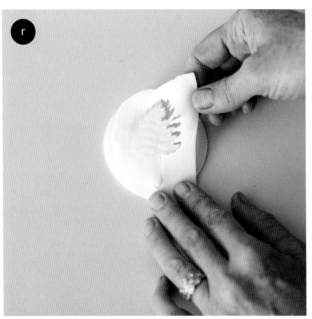

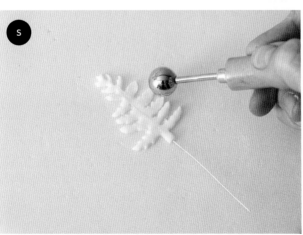

22. Arrange six pieces of fern at different heights and tape them together. Use your fingers to flare them apart a little in preparation for painting, and then paint all the ferns and their stems in silver lustre such as Flash Silver (v). Spray with edible glaze to set.

23. To make the magnolia leaves use a 5.5cm (2¼in) general leaf cutter and cut them from gumpaste rolled to 1.5mm (⅝in) thickness. Insert 24-gauge wire to around halfway into leaves. Trim the rounder end of the leaf to a more pointed shape to make them resemble a small natural magnolia leaf (w). Roll out to thin and extend, creating finished leaves around 6.5cm (2½in) in length.

24. Vein the leaves using a magnolia veiner and then use a Dresden tool to scribe the centre vein and create a natural 'v' shape. Use a balling tool to run over the edges of the leaf so they form into gentle curves, then place into bumpy foam to dry. Tape the seven leaves into a branch, with one at the top and sets of two below that. Paint the front of the leaves in gold lustre (x).

25. Paint the backs of the leaves in a dark brown lustre such as Rich Coco (y). Spray with edible glaze after painting.

26. For the large palm leaf you will need two cutters similar to a water lily petal cutter, 3cm (1⅛in) and 5cm (2in) in length, plus a middle sized cutter, 4cm(1½in) in length, which can be created by squashing a general leaf cutter with flat pliers to make it long and flat. Roll the gumpaste very thinly – it should be less than 1mm (less than 1⁄32in) – before cutting 12 of each size of leaf, 36 in total (z).

27. Insert 28-gauge wire to halfway into each leaf and use a balling tool to thin the edges and add a little shape. A couple of each size can be given a little roll with a pin to extend the length a touch. That will make a nicer transition through the sizes when they are wired together. Vein each piece with a gardenia veiner (aa) before setting to dry on bumpy foam.

28. Tape all the pieces together with white florist's tape, starting with the smallest pieces at the top and graduating down to the longest ones. Paint the assembled palm leaf in a bright yellow-gold such as Regency Gold (bb). Spray with edible glaze.

29. Airbrush the bottom cake tier with a gradient of gold through to copper (see Metallic Techniques: Airbrushing). Trim the tiers by piping fine white royal icing dots with a 1.5 writing piping nozzle (tip) and then highlight them by painting them in gold on the top two tiers and copper on the bottom tier (cc). A fine paintbrush and a bit of patience is needed for this task!

30. When arranging florals, it's generally best to start with the biggest pieces and work through to the smaller ones. The crabapple spray is the focal point so place that at the front of the top tier, with some leaves trailing down the side. Add the magnolia leaf branch to the side and seeded eucalyptus to fill the space between the two. Keep the arrangement tight and close to the surface of the tier. You don't want to be able to see visible wires and back end 'workings'. Add the palm leaf to the other side and finally the fern bunch at the back, then check for balance and harmony. Tweak and adjust any elements if needed for a more cohesive look (dd).

When arranging floral or foliage elements I don't usually work to formulas. It's good to develop an eye for what works. For example, is there an element that's too dominant? Is there an area that looks messy and doesn't 'read' nicely?

SOMETHING BLUE

These sweet fondant minis are topped with a single crabapple and palm leaf. The copper leaf 'ribbon' is not edible and should have a plastic film as a protective backing. It must be removed before serving.

Golden Regency

Gold is paired with subtle shades of grey, sage and white in this formal and regal design with a little 'Marie Antoinette' opulence. The four tiers are given interest by the addition of a gilded riser and a mix of tier shapes. Each tier has differing but complementary patterns inspired by classical architectural details.

Materials

- One pale grey fondant-covered six-petal flower shape cake tier, 26.5cm (10½in) diameter by 12.5cm (5in) tall, dowelled and stacked with foam risers (see Tip)

- Two round fondant-covered cake tiers in the following sizes: 10cm (4in) diameter by 10cm (4in) tall (pale grey fondant), and 15cm (6in) diameter by 7.5cm (3in) tall (sage green fondant), dowelled and stacked

- One white fondant-covered (sides only, not top) round foam riser, 12.5cm (5in) diameter by 2.5cm (1in) tall

- One pale grey fondant-covered round foam riser, 20cm (8in) diameter by 10cm (4in) tall

- Baking (parchment) paper

- Gumpaste, around 100g (3½oz)

- Small quantity of sugar glue

- Edible lustre powder (Faye Cahill Cake Design Lustre), Regency Gold

- Cake decorator's alcohol (95%)

- Gold leaf, 23- or 24-carat, two to three transfer sheets

- Faye Cahill Cake Design Lattice Stencil

- Wilton Wedding Jewellery Fondant Mould

- MasterMolds Old World/Victorian Banner Mould

- Prima Marketing Iron Orchid Designs Baroque #3 Mould

- Avenues Sweet Choices Chrysanthemum Border and Drop Mould

- Royal icing, around 200g (7oz)

- Florist's wire, 26-gauge white

- Large stamens

- Pasta machine

- Offset spatula

- Cutters: jasmine blossom, mini leaf, 2cm (¾in) circle, 2.5–3cm (1–1¼in) calyx, 2.5cm (1in) circle and 3cm (1¼in) 'easy blossom'

- Piping nozzle (tip), Wilton no.1, plus piping bag

- Paring knife

- Edible glaze spray

To cover the six-petal flower shape cake tier, use the following panelling method. Cover the sides first using one or more long strips of fondant (joins should be in the crease), then cover the top of the petal, cutting the fondant using a petal cake board or foam cake dummy as a template for the shape. Apply gold leaf to the sides of the small foam riser before stacking (see Metallic Techniques: Leafing). The riser should have a board underneath so that the support skewers don't poke into it once the weight of the top tiers are added. The cake may sink and become lopsided if the foam riser is not supported correctly.

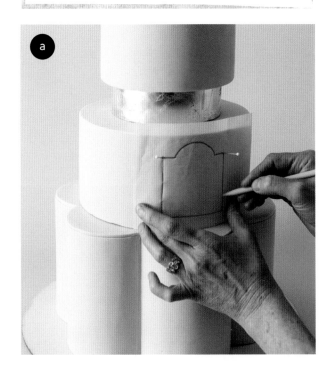

1. Trace the template (see Templates) onto baking paper (parchment paper). Position the frame on the second tier, aligning it centrally above one of the petals on the bottom tier, and pin in place. Use a scribing tool to emboss one frame above each of the six petals (a). Use the same method to emboss the loop and leaf motifs onto the petal tier, using the template (see Templates).

2. Place the lattice stencil onto the green tier, aligning the bottom edge with the bottom edge of the cake, and pin in place so that the front of the cake will have an unbroken pattern. Mask off the stencil at about 6cm (2⅜in) height using masking tape, finishing at the point of a diamond. Using a heavier mix of royal icing, spread the icing across the stencil using an offset spatula (b) and then scrape back using a flat plastic scraper. Carefully remove the stencil, wash and dry immediately, and wait around 10 minutes for the first stencil to set before pinning the stencil for the second time. Line up again, repeat and then mask off at the overlap on the other side to avoid a double image. Apply royal icing and scrape back as before. Remove the lattice stencil.

3. Roll out some white fondant to less than 3mm (⅛in) and begin passing it through a pasta machine. Use the widest setting first, and then run it through a couple more times on one of the medium settings (the exact setting will depend on the machine and also how soft or firm the fondant is). Cut some strips using the fettuccine attachment and fine 'spaghetti' attachment (c).

4. Cut 2cm (¾in) strips by hand using a ruler. Add the 2cm (¾in) strips to the lower edge of the top and bottom tiers using water to adhere. Join at the back of the top tier and in the creases of the petal tier. Use white fondant to create fine moulded strips, such as 'architectural squares' (d). Attach the moulded strips to the bottom edge of each tier, the top edge of the petal tier and the top edge of the green tier with piping gel.

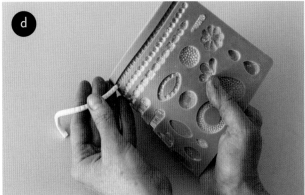

5. Attach the strips of fondant cut with the fettuccine attachment with piping gel. These strips are applied above the 'architectural squares' trim on the bottom and top tiers, leaving a small gap of around 3mm (⅛in) between the mould and the strip. Use these strips again on the top edge of the petal tier below the top moulding and above the lower moulding of the third tier. Keep the joins at the back or in the creases of the petal.

6. Place a fettuccine strip at the top edge of the stencil on the green tier (e) and add a trim of the square border aligned at the top edge of the fettuccine strip. Add a fettuccine strip over the loop of the bottom tier and neatly cut away where it overlaps. Use the fettuccine strips to create the frames too, using neat angled cuts at the joins. Use the fine spaghetti strips beside each loop on the petal tier to create the lines for the leaf motifs.

7. Make marks in the riser that align with the six creases of the petal. Apply a swag drop from the MasterMolds Old World/Victorian Banner mould at each point and then join the swags with a flower garland mould from Iron Orchid Designs Baroque #3 mould (f). On the tier with the frames, place a group of three moulded flowers from the Avenues Sweet Choices Chrysanthemum Border and Drop mould at the top of each frame plus a single flower cut from the same mould at the mid-point between each frame, as well as at the join of the leaf motifs in the crease of the petal tier.

8. Cut blossoms from thin fondant or gumpaste using a jasmine cutter and separate the flowers into individual petals using a paring knife (g). Apply these petals at the end and either side of the thin line on the bottom tier to finish the leaf motifs. Repeat this process to create the petals for the leaf garlands on the third tier. This time use white gumpaste and shape each petal into a cupped shape using a balling tool on a foam pad (h).

9. Pipe a larger dot at the junction of the lattice lines of the stencil and then a smaller one at the centre of each diamond. Use a no.1 tip for both dots, squeezing out more volume for bigger dots and less for the smaller dots (i). Highlight the stencil, larger dots and trims on the green tier, as well as the garlands on the riser, third tier and leaf embellishment on the bottom tier in Regency Gold lustre powder mixed with alcohol as a paint (j).

10. Roll gumpaste to approximately 1mm (¹⁄₃₂in) and cut around 18 blossom shapes using the 'easy blossom' cutter. Keep the cut blossoms covered and work with three or four at a time, using a balling tool to thin out and add shape to the petals. Keep the centre section thicker (k).

11. Secure a large stamen to the 26-gauge white wire with florist's tape. Attach the blossom to the stamen using sugar glue, positioning so that the petals curve outwards (l). Work with your fingers to close up the join and shape the lower section into a neat tapered cone. Leave overnight to dry.

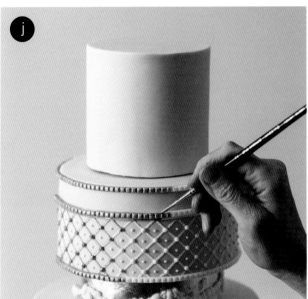

The cupped petals on the tier with the frames are easier to apply using royal icing piped with a no.1 nozzle (tip). Start with the ones on either side of the single flower and work back to the group of three flowers to create a swag shape. Overlap the petals and leaves slightly, and pipe dots where needed to fill any gaps.

12. Roll white gumpaste to 1mm (1/32in), and cut 25–30 mini leaves. Cut the 26-gauge white florist's wire into quarters and insert into the end of each leaf. Apply a tiny amount of sugar glue on the tip of the wire before inserting (m). Gently roll out the leaf a little more to increase the size and thin the edges. Use a leaf embosser to add veining and leave overnight to dry (n). Wire together five of these tiny leaves into sprigs.

13. Cut the 26-gauge wire into quarters and hook one end. Add a pea-size ball of gumpaste using sugar glue and leave overnight to dry. Roll white gumpaste to very thin on the pasta machine and cut nine 2cm (3/4in) diameter circles (three for each rose). Roll again to extend to around 3cm (1 1/4in) diameter and thin the edges. Attach one petal to the ball, creating a pointed spiral. Work with a paintbrush to close the centre so that the ball is not visible (o).

14. Add two more of the same size petals either side and fold back the edges with your fingers to create a rose bud (p). Add a calyx to the one that will be used on the top tier of the cake using a calyx cutter approximately 2.5–3cm (1–1 1/4in) wide. Leave overnight to dry or put into a dehydrator for an hour. Leave the three that will become full size roses without a calyx.

15. Roll out a thin layer of white gumpaste and cut 15 circles, 2.5cm (1in) diameter, (five for each rose). Roll out each one further to thin the edges and increase the size to around 4cm (1 5/8in) diameter. Lay over the rounded back of a paint palette and gently fold back the top edge on two sides (q). Leave all five petals to dry slightly until they hold their shape but are still a little flexible.

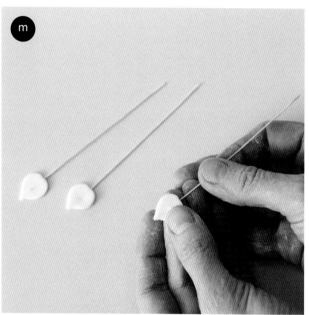

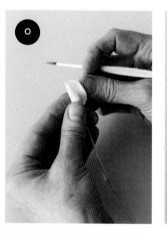

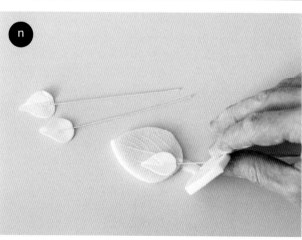

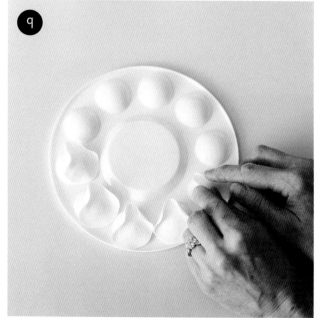

16. Attach the petals to the rose bud using sugar glue, overlapping each petal by half on the previous petal (r). Leave overnight to dry or use a dehydrator. Paint all blossoms, leaves and roses in Regency Gold, including the stems, and then apply edible glaze spray to set the lustre so it will not shake off the flowers. Arrange the three large roses a little to one side on the top tier of the cake and then add leaf sprigs and blossoms to form an asymmetric arrangement with the rose bud falling down to the front.

ELEGANT SUGAR COOKIES

What a gorgeous way to incorporate the details of this cake onto dessert table treats! These round cookies have been iced in pale grey and sage green, then detailed in gold and white with elements from the centrepiece cake: lattice stencil, moulded flowers and delicate leaves.

Champagne Bubbles

Strong and sleek underneath with a burst of lightweight bubbles on top, this striking look comes from the precision of the stripes combined with the unexpected fun of the bubbles. To nail this design, it's important that the tiers have been ganached and covered perfectly to have a sharp and tailored shape.

Materials

- Two round white fondant-covered cake tiers, dowelled and stacked, in the following sizes: 20cm (8in) diameter by 7.5cm (3in) tall and 23cm (9in) diameter by 10cm (4in) tall

- White fondant, 200g (7oz)

- Black fondant, 200g (7oz)

- Stripe templates made from thin cardboard, at least 75cm (30in) long and cut to the following sizes: stripe one – 1.5cm (⅝in), stripe two – 2cm (¾in), stripe three – 3cm (1¼in), stripe four – 4.5cm (1¾in), stripe five – 6cm (2⅜in), stripe six – 7.5cm (3in), stripe seven – 9cm (3½in), stripe eight – 10cm (4in)

- Edible pen

- Pasta machine

- Royal icing, 100g (3½oz)

- Sharp paring knife

- Acetate buffer

- Edible lustre powders (Faye Cahill Cake Design Lustre), Copper, Bronze, Regency Gold and Shimmer Gold, Pearl White

- Fine paintbrush and fluffy brushes

- Gelatin crystals

- Water balloons and hand pump

- Florist's wire, 24-gauge

- White vegetable fat (shortening)

- Florist's tape

- Clear alcohol, such as vodka

1. The stripes will be much easier to apply if the cakes and cake board are covered the day before to allow the fondant to become firm. The top surfaces of the pre-covered cakes will be visible on the finished cake, but the sides will be overlaid with stripes, so don't worry about pin holes or smudges on the sides. Decide where the back of the cake will be and mark two vertical lines with an edible pen (a). Use the edge of something like a scraper to keep your line straight. This will be where the stripes will start and finish.

2. Roll out some white fondant in a pasta machine. Start by rolling the fondant by hand to 3–4mm (⅛in), then thin the fondant down to one of the mid-settings, like 3 or 4, by passing it though the widest setting of the machine. Pass it through a couple more times while narrowing the setting. The finished sheets should be at least 75cm (30in) long. Repeat this process with the black fondant. Cut the fondants into strips around 2.5cm (1in) wide (b). This first cut is a rough cut and does not need to be measured but it helps to have the cuts nice and smooth.

3. Roll up each strip and set aside (c). You will need seven white strips and nine black. Keep the rolls of fondant covered so they don't dry out.

a

4. Brush some water onto a section of the cake that you will be applying stripes to (d). If I am doing a cake with the same sequence of stripes on more than one tier, I will apply each stripe on all tiers before moving to the next tier. It's much quicker than working one tier at a time.

5. Start with the bottom stripe. Beginning at the line that marks the back of the cake, uncurl a roll of black fondant around the base of the cake. Cut neatly to join at the back (e). Make sure the stripe is flush with the tier below or the base board. Push it down if necessary, and give it a polish with an acetate buffer to smooth it out.

6. Wrap the narrowest stripe template (stripe one) around the base of the cake, securing it at the back with pins. Do a check around to make sure it is flush with the bottom of the tier or cake board. Trim the fondant to the height of the template. It's important to hold the knife as level as possible. Angling it up or down can produce an imperfect line. Remove the excess fondant above the template and then take off the cardboard strip (f).

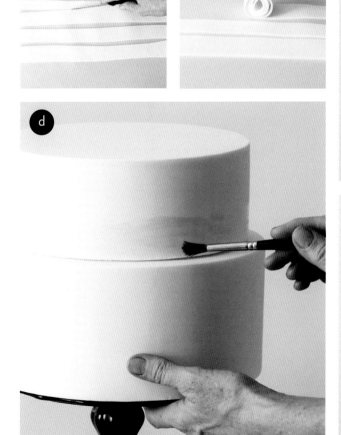

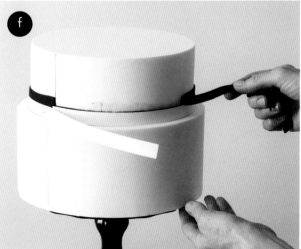

7. Wet another section of the tier and add a strip of white (g). Again do a check to make sure the stripe is flush with the one below. It can help to get down at eye level while doing this as very small gaps are hard to see from above. Wrap the template for stripe two around the cake and trim the excess white. Each template strip will sit flush to the base of the tier or cake board – the height of the template is calculated to be the total width of the stripes to that point. For example, template number two is the added widths of stripes one and two. Template number three is the added widths of stripes one, two and three.

8. Next add another strip in black fondant, having trimmed stripe two (h). Buff over the stripes applied so far, using the acetate buffer, to smooth them and meld them together.

9. Pin the template for stripe three to the cake (i), trim the black fondant to size and remove the excess.

10. Remove template three (j), then add another white strip of fondant. Continue this method to the top of the tier. For the last stripe, use the top edge of the tier as a guide to cutting and trim so the strip is flush with the top edge. The top tier is not as tall as the base so you will only need to use the first six templates. The lower tier will need templates seven and eight as well.

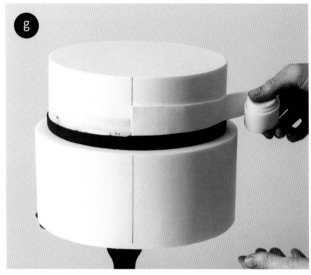

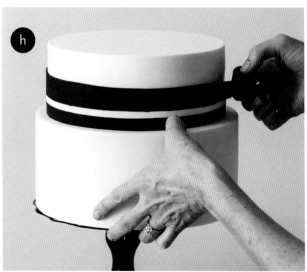

11. Use florist's tape to mask the stripes and make them quicker to paint. Start by making a few small folds at one end of the tape and pinning it to the cake through the thicker folded section. This will stop the tape from tearing as you stretch it. Wrap it around the lower edge of the stripe to be painted, stretching it a little to keep it tight and firmly in place. Make a few folds again to create a thicker section before pinning it at back of the cake where it meets the start of the tape. Do the same on the upper edge of the stripe (k).

12. Make a thickish mix of alcohol and edible lustre powder for each metallic colour. The alcohol in this case can be vodka or another lower percentage spirit. The water content will create a stickiness that will stop the lustre powder from shedding when dry. Paint the area of each stripe and remove the tape (l). Touch up any unpainted areas using a very fine brush. Any smudges can be removed with a light brush of water and a dab with a tissue. The bottom white stripe is painted Copper on each tier and the white stripe above that is painted Bronze on both. The bottom tier also has the top white stripe painted in Regency Gold, leaving each tier with one unpainted white stripe.

13. For the gelatin bubbles, use water balloons inflated with a hand pump to sizes around 2.5–4cm (1–1½in) diameter. Sometimes when inflated the balloon will have a visible peak or 'nipple'. If the shape of the inflated balloon does not look round enough, squeeze some air into that area using hand pressure and roll it around until the shape looks better. Secure a small length of florist's wire to the knot of the balloon, then apply a thin film of white vegetable fat (shortening) all over (m). Make around 60 balloons for this cake.

14. Make a gelatin mixture using four tablespoons of gelatin crystals and eight tablespoons of water. Add ½ teaspoon of Pearl White lustre powder and mix. Microwave for 10–20 seconds at a time until the gelatin is dissolved. At this stage it may be too hot to dip the balloons into straight away so allow it to cool a little. It's a good idea to have a bowl of very hot water on hand for this process, as the mixture will cool very quickly and become 'gluggy'. If this happens, stand the bowl of mixture in hot water so it becomes workable again. Dip the balloon, rolling it around until fully covered (n).

15. Hold the coated balloon over the bowl and allow excess to drip off (o). It can help to have a skewer on hand to gently remove the final drops which will be beginning to thicken. If they are not removed before setting, they will be permanent and spoil the shape. Hang the bubbles on a flower drying rack, a clothes airer, or from wire shelving bars to dry overnight, using the wire to help secure them.

16. The next day, pop the balloon with a pin and remove the remains of the wire and balloon with tweezers (p).

17. Dust edible lustres over the bubbles with a fluffy brush (q). This dry brushing technique will give a softer tint and retain the transparency of the balloon. I used Shimmer Gold, Bronze and Regency Gold for this cake. Some bubbles can be left clear.

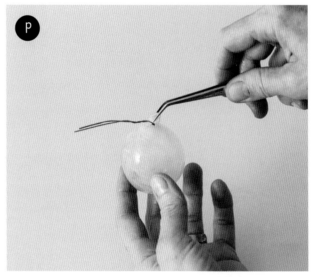

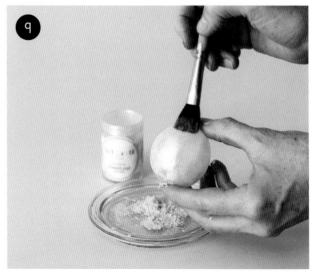

18. Not all the bubbles will be perfect, so start arranging the less perfect ones in the centre of the cake and save the best ones for the outside. Create a mound of bubbles, using royal icing to secure each one in place (r). Work carefully on the arrangement so the open end of the bubble is not visible and the royal icing dots cannot be seen either. Pile the better bubbles on top of the less perfect ones to make a nice high and full topper.

CAKE JAR

A cute and delicious cake jar with layers of chocolate bourbon cake and spiced marscapone makes a great dessert portion version of this cake. Top it with a gelatin bubble and candy-covered chocolate balls in black and gold.

Woodland Crown

An enchanted confection, the Woodland Crown is created by combining a gilded bark effect with a floral garland in muted tones with a hint of sparkle. The natural elements have a delicate beauty that is elevated to a magical quality by the addition of metallics, gold and glitter. Decide how the finished cake will be viewed before choosing whether to position the crown on the top or on the side.

Materials

- One round white fondant-covered cake, 15cm (6in) diameter and 7.5cm (3in) tall
- Dark grey fondant, 100g (3½oz)
- Pasta machine
- Gumpaste, 150g (5½oz)
- Sugar glue
- Silver leaf, five transfer sheets
- Florist's wire, 28-, 26-, 24- and 22-gauge white
- Wire cutters and long-nose pliers
- Florist's tape, white and green
- Five lily stamens and one large ball stamen
- Dahlia centre silicone mould
- Cutters: 4.5cm (1¾in) 12-petal daisy, 3.5cm (1⅜in) cosmos petal, five-petal jasmine blossom, 1.5cm (⅝in) general leaf (for jasmine vine), 4.5cm (1¾in) 10-petal daisy and 5.5cm (2¼in) lily/waterlily petal
- General leaf veiner
- Liquid colours, black, green, teal, brown and orange
- Cake decorator's alcohol (95%)
- Petal dusts, grey, green, dusty peach, and dusty purple
- Edible lustre powder (Faye Cahill Cake Design Lustre), Regency Gold
- Fluffy brush
- Edible glitter (Faye Cahill Cake Design, All That Glitters)

1. Start by making the bark effect for the cake side. Create the dark grey fondant by mixing pre-coloured black fondant into white, or you can knead black gel paste into white fondant. The bark can be created in one long strip, however, two shorter ones will be a little easier to handle, and the joins will not be noticeable if they are torn by hand rather than cut with a knife. The full strip should be around 50cm (20in) long (or you can make two 25cm (10in) sections) and 8cm (3¼in) wide. Roll out the grey fondant in a pasta machine to around 2mm (1⁄16in) thick and then cut it to size. Apply silver leaf along the full strip (see Metallic Techniques: Leafing) (a).

Large ball stamens are a product I find many uses for. They can be coloured and used as fillers like berries or, as here, as the structure on which to build a larger flower. An alternative would be to dry a pea-sized ball of gumpaste on a hooked wire and use that as the base for this flower centre.

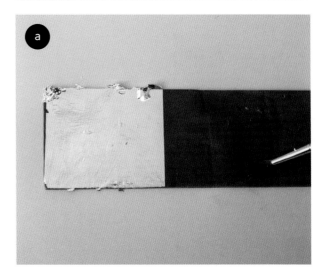

2. Use a small rolling pin to stretch out the strip, which will have the effect of breaking up the solid silver leaf and creating crackled and crazed areas (b). Some of the silver may stick to the rolling pin and come off. A little of that is fine as you want to see some areas of grey, but if too much comes off, you can re-apply more silver onto any areas that need it.

3. Tear along one short edge to enable you to create a more natural join, and trim back any curves in the long edges caused by the stretching so the strip will again fit the side of the cake perfectly. Wet the cake side with water and attach the finished bark. Tear off any excess where the pieces join and gently press down to integrate the seam in the fondant (c).

4. The feature flower of this wreath is a stylised bloom, not a particular botanical type, and combines the centre of a dahlia and petals similar to a double cosmos flower. Build the centre on a large ball stamen. To give the stem strength, tape a length of 22-gauge wire to the stamen (d).

5. Use a silicone mould to make the dahlia centre, then unmould the gumpaste and attach it to the ball stamen with sugar glue. Completely wrap the flower centre around the ball stamen and pinch it to secure it underneath for a good strong seal (e). If you don't have a dahlia centre mould, cover a ball stamen thickly with gumpaste and then cut in some fine snips using pointed scissors.

6. Roll out gumpaste to 1mm ($1/_{32}$ in) or less. Use a 12-petal daisy cutter, about 4.5cm (1¾in) in diameter, or something similar, to cut two pieces and then use a balling tool to thin and shape the petals (f). This is a very delicate and fragile shape, but if you lose a petal or two it's never noticeable.

7. Paint sugar glue on the underside of the flower centre, keeping it light by blotting the brush after dipping in the glue. Too much will cause slippage and take too long to dry. Then thread the daisy pieces onto the centre and secure them one at a time (g). Allow the tiny petals to sit loosely and naturally around the centre. When both layers are added, hang the flower centre upside down to dry, bending the wire into a hook to hang it up by.

8. Roll out some gumpaste to around 1.5mm (⅝in) thick and cut the petals using a 3.5cm (1⅜in) cosmos petal cutter. You will need 14 for the flower, but make a few extras to allow for breakage. Cut each full length piece of 26-gauge wire into four to make shorter lengths, then insert one to about halfway through each petal (h). Use a little sugar glue to stick the wires in if necessary, but you may not need it if the gumpaste is quite sticky.

9. Use a small rolling pin to extend and thin the petal a little, avoiding the wire as much as possible (i). The finished petal should be around 4cm (1½in)

10. Press the petal using either a poppy or cosmos veiner (j).

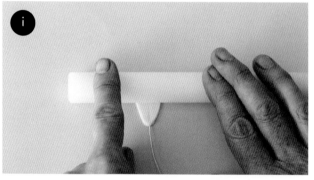

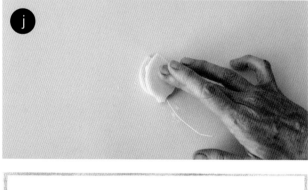

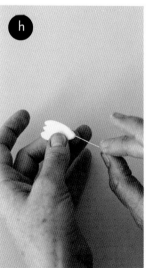

If using sugar glue to stick leaves to wires, I dip the wire so it barely touches the glue adding only the tiniest amount. Any more and you will be more likely to have problems with wires twisting due to the glue not setting fully.

11. Use a balling tool to create cupped shapes at the end of the petal. Also run the balling tool along both sides to work over the cut edge, thinning it out for a finer looking petal (k).

12. Lay each petal onto bumpy foam to dry overnight. Pinch the area around the wire as you lay it down to make a nicer shape on the inner side of the petal (l).

13. When both the flower centre and the petals are fully dry, assemble the flower by first taping five petals around the centre. Five will be tricky to hold at once, so tape on three and then another two. Move the petals after taping if needed so they are spaced out evenly. The second layer is formed of nine petals. Again, add three or four at a time for easier handling. Attach them as close as possible to the first layer so the whole flower is tight and compact (m). You never want to see the wires in a sugar flower.

14. The dusty peach colour of this flower is created by firstly diluting a red-based brown edible paint or airbrush colour with alcohol and then painting the flower with a colour wash technique (see Metallic Techniques: Painting). If you find that brown doesn't achieve the desired result, then a mix of orange or peach with brown or black will give a similar look. You want a 'barely there' tinge of colour (n).

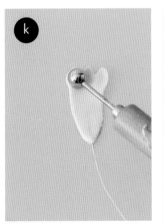

I keep all my broken white gumpaste flowers and use them as colour testers. It's very easy to go too dark if you don't test a colour first!

15. Allow the alcohol wash to dry fully, and then apply dusty peach petal dust to the centre and inner petals with a fluffy brush (o). Deepening the colour of the centre adds depth and brings out the tone of the subtle colour wash.

16. At one side of the crown are some blossom sprigs similar to a jasmine vine. The blossoms and leaves are made according to the method described in the Golden Regency cake, steps 10–12. Make three blossoms and 15 leaves. Start by taping three leaves together, using white florist's tape. Next tape in a blossom and then add two more leaves below the blossom (p). This completes one sprig and you need three in total for the crown.

17. Paint each sprig green using a spring green colour wash (q). Make this by adding a drop each of green and orange into cake decorator's alcohol. These paints keep well in sealed jars, so when I mix a green that I love, I make sure to save it! Leave the front of the blossom white and paint everything else including all wires and taped stems in the green.

18. Tape together the three sprigs, offsetting each one so it sits below the one it's being attached to (r). Paint all the new joins in the same green as the leaves.

19. The group of dusty purple blossoms are stylised wild daisies and you need to make five for this cake. Start by taking a large lily stamen and reinforce it by taping a length of 24-gauge wire to it with green florist's tape (s). Make sure it's taped right into the hard stamen head or the finished daisy flower will not be supported well.

20. Roll gumpaste to 1mm (1/32in) thick and cut one blossom shape per flower with a five-petal jasmine cutter, 3cm (1 1/8in) in diameter. If you don't have one of these, any similar cutter with five or six petals will be fine. Use a balling tool to thin and cup three of the petals and then turn over and do the same to the remaining two petals so they curve in the opposite direction (t). Aim to achieve a 'messy' look with this flower.

21. Paint a tiny amount of sugar glue around the stamen head then thread the blossom on. Pinch to secure and hang the blossom upside down to dry. Notice how cupping the petals in different directions makes them sit in a more random, natural way (u).

22. The second layer of petals is made with a 4.5cm (1¾in) 10-petal daisy cutter from 1mm (1⁄32in) gumpaste. Every second petal is shaped with the balling tool and then the piece is flipped over and the alternate petals are shaped in the opposite direction. Add sugar glue to the base of the dried centre you made in step 20, and thread on the second layer. Gently scrunch and squeeze the soft gumpaste so it adheres to the centre and the petals fall outwards nicely (v). The scrunching process may cause some petals to overlap which is fine for this flower and adds to the wild effect. Dry in a cupped flower former or make a hole for the wire in some bumpy foam and set it to dry overnight.

23. The colour wash for this flower is made by adding the tiniest bit of black liquid into an alcohol base. Put a drop of black airbrush colour into a palette and then very lightly dip the edge of your paintbrush into it to pick up the small quantity of black you need. If your diluted black lacks the lovely dusty purple black colour required, you can achieve this colour by combining purple and black. Paint the full flower with this colour wash and allow to dry (w). When fully dry, dust some petal dust in a stronger dusty purple into the centre.

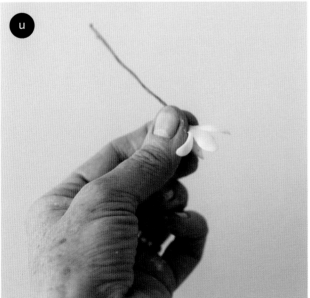

24. Tape together the five daisies so they sit at different heights. Start by joining three, then add the remaining two below. Trim the wire short after taping (x).

25. The making of the fern pieces is described in the Fall Foliage cake, steps 18–22. You will need five pieces of fern for this cake. Tape them together at slightly different heights and then use your fingers to flare the pieces apart in preparation for painting. The fern is painted in a colour wash made by combining teal and black liquid colour in a base of alcohol (y).

26. Next cut seven eucalyptus leaves using a 5.5cm (2¼in) lily/waterlily petal cutter. Insert a 24-gauge wire about halfway into the leaf, then roll with a small rolling pin to extend and thin the leaf to around 7cm (2¾in) long. Vein using a general leaf veiner and then take one or two nicks out of the side of the leaf using the pointed end of another cutter (z). Finally, lay the leaves on bumpy foam to dry.

27. Tape together the seven leaves, using white florist's tape, at different heights and paint with an alcohol wash tinted with teal, green and black liquid colour (aa).

28. Now you are ready to create the garland crown. Use a double thickness of 24-gauge wire, taped together with florist's tape. First line up two wires next to each other, plus a third one halfway offset (bb).

29. Tape over the area that has the double wire and then add more wires at each end so that a long length is created with double wire throughout. Make a very long piece, about four wires in length (cc). Then join the single ends together into a full circle by taping them together. The completed circle will be bigger than the cake, so add a few twists, folds and loops to reduce the size so it sits nicely at the edge of the top surface of your cake.

30. Now create a vine effect with a few more lengths of taped wire, made using two 24-gauge wires and white tape. Start adding these wires to the garland by taping and twisting them together. Make some areas more dense with vine, and have some lighter sections. Paint the garland a neutral grey-brown using a mixture of petal dust and alcohol (dd).

31. Now you can start adding the flowers and leaves. First trim the wires short on all the pieces and then bend the large flower stem back on itself before taping it to the vine (ee).

32. Because you are taping the flowers to a circle, use a wrapping motion rather than the twisting one you would use for taping straight elements together. Use short lengths of florist's tape and make sure to pull the tape firmly while wrapping (ff). The stretching releases the adhesive inside the tape to make it stick securely. Tuck the bunch of daisies next to the large bloom and tape in place. Keep everything nice and tight with overlaps that hide the taping and the back end structure of the sugar flowers.

33. Leave a gap on the other side of the large flower and secure the blossom sprigs. Fill the gap by adding the fern leaves between flower and sprigs of blossom. Finally tape the eucalyptus leaves in place at the other end of the arrangement (gg). Paint any visible tape in the grey-brown paint to integrate it.

34. Highlight the edges of all flowers and leaves with Regency Gold lustre dust. Every piece should be highlighted to some degree, but leave some parts of each element without highlighter too. Use a light touch to achieve an organic and natural effect (hh).

35. Dab some gel randomly over the arrangement and apply edible glitter to those areas. The glitter does not have to be on every leaf and flower. Use a little more on the larger flower, especially in the centre, and then scattered a little more over the rest of the arrangement including all the blossom and daisy centres and some of the leaves (ii).

This crown will rest on the cake without needing to be secured to it, so there will be no need to pierce holes in the cake or use protective barriers that are needed when florist's wires go into cakes. If support is needed, add a small ball of wetted, tacky fondant behind the large flower to keep it in place. For transport, the crown should travel separately, packed with tissue surrounding it.

To make the most impact, you want everyone to be able to see the whole of your floral crown. This means you should choose whether the crown is placed on top or to the side of the cake. Think about how the cake will be viewed: if it will be displayed on a dessert table it will be mainly seen from the side. In a more intimate gathering it might be placed in the centre of a table, and viewed from above.

RUSTIC ALMOND RINGS

Pretty almond dainties make a sweet accompaniment to the Woodland Crown cake. These gluten-free treats have been decorated with white sugar blossoms as well as vines and leaves piped in royal icing.

Blush & Gold Colour Block

The Blush & Gold Colour Block cake uses the textures of edible gold and lustre over its tall, tailored shape. The focus of this cake is a large soft bloom, my signature 'peony rose'. It's a refined, light looking flower, with both a stylised and natural appearance, and it's surprisingly quick to make.

Materials

- Two white fondant-covered cake tiers, as follows: one round 10cm (4in) diameter by 12.5cm (5in) tall, and one 12.5cm (5in) square by 18cm (7in) tall

- Gold leaf, 23- or 24-carat, eight transfer sheets

- Lemon gold leaf, four transfer sheets

- Gumpaste, around 100g (3½oz)

- Pasta machine

- Sugar glue

- Florist's wire, 18-gauge, one piece, and 24-gauge, two to three pieces

- Wire cutters

- Foam ball, 4cm (1½in) diameter

- Circle cutters, 4cm (1½in) and 4.5cm (1¾in)

- Waterlily petal cutter, 5.5cm (2¼in) long

- Hot glue gun

- Piping gel

- Edible marker and ruler

- Patty or muffin trays or apple trays, to use as flower former

- Cake decorator's alcohol (95%)

- Petal dust, cream

- Fluffy brush

- Edible lustre powders (Faye Cahill Cake Design Lustre), Shimmer Gold, Regency Gold and Powder Pink

- Edible glitter (Faye Cahill Cake Design, All That Glitters)

1. Start by making the peony rose two days before decorating the cake, or use a dehydrator to speed up the process. Begin by cutting an 18-gauge wire into thirds and securing one third into a 4cm (1½in) foam ball with hot glue (a). Pierce the hole first, then add glue and re-insert the wire into the hole for maximum strength. This flower will be large and heavy and needs a stable base.

2. Roll gumpaste to around 2–3mm (1⁄16–1⁄8in) in the pasta machine and cut two 4cm (1½in) circles. Thin and extend these circles by rolling them out by hand to around 7cm (2¾in) diameter. Turn a couple of times during rolling to keep the shape regular. Cut both circles in half (b). For one flower you only need three of these half-circles. Usually I would be making multiple flowers at one time so the extra does not go to waste!

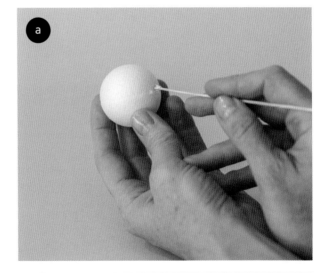

3. Paint the upper half of the foam ball with sugar glue. Use just a very thin coat, or you will have problems with the gumpaste slipping and melting. It can help with handling to let the gumpaste petals dry very slightly before positioning them. If they are too floppy, it's hard to get the shape right. Lay the first petal across the ball so that the highest point of the semi-circle sits over the centre of the foam ball and forms a gentle peak (c). The peak should be aligned vertically to the florist's wire stem.

4. Add a little sugar glue to one side of the first petal before attaching the second one. You are aiming to offset each petal by a third so that they are equally spaced. Add glue to the side of the second petal before attaching the third (d).

5. Attach the third petal and lift the edge of the first petal to tuck it in so all the overlaps are in the same direction (e). Smooth down any loose gumpaste on the underside of the bud. At this stage the top half of the ball should be covered.

6. Cut another five circles of gumpaste with the 4cm (1½in) cutter and roll them out to around 8cm (3¼in). The edges should be nice and thin from the rolling process. Place the five petals into a patty or muffin tray, or into an apple tray. There should be a flat section for one third of the petal which will be the base and the rest should naturally form into soft folds which will be the upper part of the petals (f). Leave the petals to semi-dry. They are ready when they hold their shape but are still a little pliable, not hard and crispy. This can take 10 minutes or more, depending on the gumpaste and conditions.

7. Paint the lower half of the bud with sugar glue, as always, using the glue sparingly, then start adding the medium petals by applying the first one to the side of the ball (g). It should sit so the petal finishes higher than the centre. The positioning is more to the side than underneath, think about applying it to the widest part of the ball.

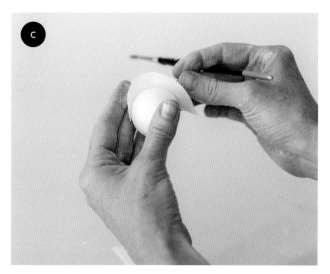

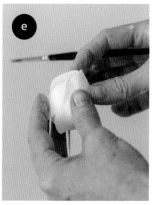

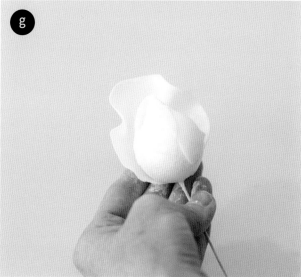

8. Paint a little sugar glue at the lower part and to the side of the first petal. The glue should not extend up the full edge of the petal, only apply it near the base (h).

9. Tuck in the second petal so it overlaps by half on the first petal and press firmly to secure (i). Then paint a dab of glue in the same spot of the second petal.

10. Continue adding petals. At the fourth addition, the first and fourth petal should roughly meet; this will tell you that the spacing is correct and the fifth petal can be added so it overlaps by half inside the fourth petal and then wraps over the first petal, also overlapping by half (j). Press very firmly round the base of the flower to secure all of the medium petals.

11. The rose will look more beautiful and integrated if one side of each petal sits closer to the centre and one side flares to the outside. Tuck a little tissue on the same side of each petal to flare it out, then hang upside down to dry overnight (if you have a dehydrator, I find they can be dried in around an hour) (k).

12. Cut six gumpaste circles using the 4.5cm (1¾in) cutter. Roll and extend each one until it is very fine and measures around 9.5cm (3¾in) in diameter. These petals should be semi-dried over the rounded side of the patty or muffin tray or apple tray (l). For this stage there is no particular shape required, just drape them loosely over and wait until they hold their shape.

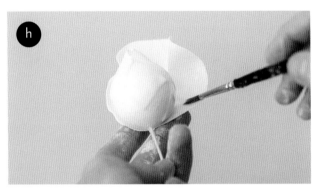

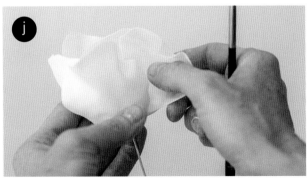

13. Paint the lower section of the rose lightly with sugar glue then attach petals as before. They should finish at the height of the medium petals with each one overlapping by half (m). This stage gets a little awkward to handle. I still prefer to hold the flower upright, but if needed you can flip it over and overlay the petals rather than tucking them on the inside.

14. Again, check the spacing when adding the second last petal. The first and fifth petals should roughly meet, allowing you to tuck in the sixth petal so it overlaps by half on the previous one and then wraps over the first petal by half (n). Turn upside down and firmly press around the base to secure all petals.

15. Add tissue to one side of each petal to support and shape it while it dries. As before, one side of each petal sits closer to the centre and one side flares out (o). Hang upside down to dry overnight, or in dehydrator for an hour.

16. Using a fluffy brush, dust cream petal dust into the centre of the flower (p). Then hold it upside down and tap out any excess.

17. Paint some piping gel along some of the inner petal edges. Dab glitter onto the gel using a dry paintbrush (q) and then shake out any excess.

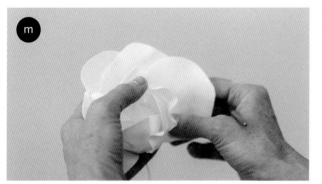

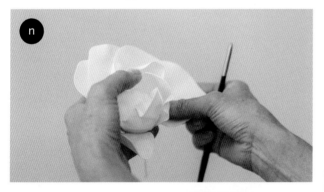

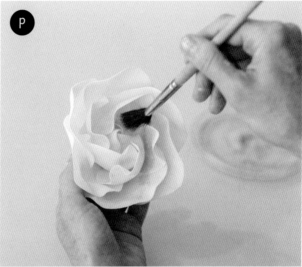

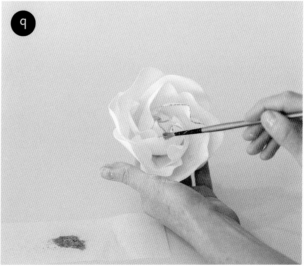

18. Next add the lustre finish to the cake tiers. Lustre the top tier in Powder Pink and the top third of the sides of the bottom tier in Shimmer Gold (see Metallic Techniques: Applying Lustre). This should be done before stacking to allow you to more easily apply the gold leaf on the top surface of the tall square tier. Using an edible marker and ruler, mark in an angled line roughly a third of the way down the bottom tier. The angle is only a little off from horizontal, nothing too dramatic. Continue this around all four sides and join at the front (r).

19. Remove the lustre that is below the line by carefully painting on a little water and then blotting it off with a tissue, otherwise the lustre will prevent the leaf from adhering. To get the sharpest line at the top and bottom of the gold section, cut pieces of leaf that include a straight edge. Apply the leaf (see Metallic Techniques: Leafing) taking care to line up the straight edge of the leaf with the marked line on the cake (s). Fill in the area below with more leaf leaving the bottom third uncovered.

20. Wash off any excess lustre on the top surface of the square tier using the blotting method described in step 19, and apply lemon gold leaf to the surface. You are aiming to get a nice sharp square, so make use of the perfect corners and lines on the sheets of leaf, lining them up with the edges of the square (t).

21. Dowel the bottom tier and stack on the top tier (see General Techniques: Dowelling & Stacking), then mark out the next set of lines over the gold leaf (u). Again these are shallow, not sharp angled lines.

22. Paint piping gel over the last third of the bottom tier. Start by using a fine brush at the top line and then switch to a larger brush to fill out the whole area. Make sure no areas are left dry, but don't use too much gel either. You want good thin and even coverage. Tip out some edible glitter near the base of the cake, and then use a soft fluffy brush to dust it up onto the sticky gelled section. Work carefully to make sure there is solid coverage of glitter (v).

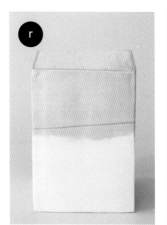

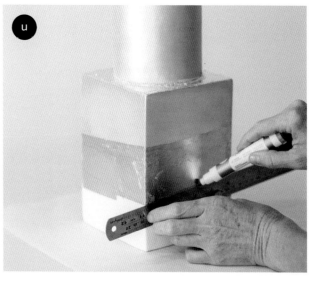

23. To finish the glitter in a straight line at the top, hold a ruler against the cake to mask off the gold leaf, then continue dusting the glitter up to and against the ruler (w). After the glitter is applied, dust away the excess from the base and spray the cake with edible glaze, making sure the glitter section is very well covered.

24. Position the flower offset to the side of the cake and angled upwards a little. The gum leaves have been made according to the method in the Woodland Crown cake, steps 26–27. Make six or seven and tape them together with florist's tape. Paint in Regency Gold to highlight them and spray with edible glaze before setting them on the cake, as shown (x).

COLOUR BLOCK CAKESICLES

Cakesicles are a super-cute update on the cake pops trend. These red-velvet filled confections have been dipped in Candy Melts and decorated with lustre and glitter in colour block style.

General Techniques

Assembling

The foundation of a beautiful cake is perfectly shaped and covered tiers, as well as proper construction. A poorly supported cake can tilt and sink while on display, while good construction will allow your carefully prepared decorations to shine through the entire event. The following pages will tell you how to go about making the perfect base for your designs. The first step is to layer and crumb coat the cake with ganache. This has the practical effect of making each cake tier the desired height and providing the perfect surface for fondant, but also allows you to introduce mouth-watering flavours in the fillings.

MATERIALS

- Sturdy cake boards in your required sizes, for this example two boards for each of the following tier sizes: 10cm (4in), 15cm (6in) and 20cm (8in)

- MDF base board, larger than the bottom tier, a cake this size needs a 25cm (10in) board

- Additional working board or food board for each tier of cake, larger than cake tier size

- Baked cakes of the sizes required, for a 10cm (4in) finished cake height, for example, you need each cake to be 7.5cm (3in) high

- White chocolate ganache (see Recipes)

- Flavouring, optional (in this case, freeze-dried passionfruit powder)

- Simple syrup

- Pastry brush

- Serrated knife or cake leveller

- Palette knife

- Flat scraper

- Fine paring knife

- Ruler and right angle

- 12mm (½in) dowel

- Power drill and drill bits, 12mm (½in) and 16mm (⅝in)

- Masking tape

- Hot glue gun

- Template for finding centre of circle

1. Find the centre of each of your tier boards and base board. To make a template for this, use a square board and draw diagonal lines corner to corner. From the centre, mark out 1.25cm or half-inch increments along each line. Number each increment mark starting at one and continuing for the length of the line (a). For example, the point marked '5' will be 6.25cm or 2½in from the centre. The full 12.5cm or 5in comes from adding the two increments that are either side of the centre.

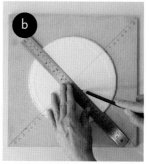
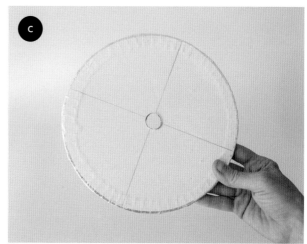

2. Position your circular cake board so it sits within its diameter-size marking. If the cake board does not exactly match the template increment marks, move it so the markers are equal distances at all points. Draw a cross on the cake board that lines up with the cross of the template board and the centre is where the lines intersect (b). Repeat for all the tier cake boards.

3. Drill a hole in each of the cake boards that is larger than the dowel size (c). If you are using 12mm (½in) dowel, drill a 16mm (⅝in) hole in the cake boards. This allows you to move the tier if necessary after stacking in case it is not perfectly centred.

4. Apply some softened white chocolate ganache to the food board or working board and press the tier board firmly on to adhere it. Having the cake firmly stuck to a base board during ganache and covering will make the process much easier. Use white chocolate regardless of cake flavour as there is less danger of smudges during stacking than when using dark chocolate (d).

5. Find the centre of the base board and drill a hole the same width as the dowel. Use a 12mm (½in) dowel and drill a 12mm (½in) hole (e). On the underside of the board, add some masking tape across the hole to prevent glue from coming through.

6. Cut the dowel to the length required. The base should be cut straight and the top on an angle to make stacking easier. The height is calculated by adding together the finished heights of the bottom two tiers plus half of the height of the top tier. Add extra for the thickness of the base board if needed. For this example you have three 10cm (4in) tiers so the dowel should be 10+10+5cm=25cm (4+4+2=10in). If you are using a double-thickness board for the base board (see step 8) add on 2cm (¾in) and make the pole 27cm (10¾in) from the straight cut base end to the highest point on the angled end. Sand off any splinters (f) and wash thoroughly or use cake decorator's alcohol to sanitise.

7. Apply hot glue to the base of the dowel (g) and immediately push the dowel into the drilled hole (h).

8. A single board is sufficient to carry the weight of even a very heavy cake, but a double-thickness board can be used to make the board look more substantial and allows you to use some nicer ribbons to trim it. You can create a double board by securing two singles together with hot glue before drilling the centre hole.

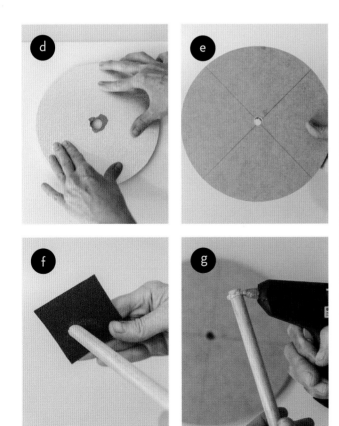

9. Take one of your baked cakes and trim the top level. A small rounded section may be left around the edge so that you don't waste too much cake in the trimming (i). You need 7.5cm (3in) of cake height for this example cake. If your cake has baked higher, you don't necessarily have to trim all the excess and waste it. If it's the bottom tier, you can allow it to be a little higher than planned. However, only make upper tiers higher if they will not finish taller than the bottom tier – that would look disproportional.

10. With the cake on a turntable, use a serrated knife or cake leveller to split it into 2.5cm (1in) layers (j). Use a sawing motion while rotating the cake for best results. If needed, you can measure and mark points with a cocktail stick (toothpick) to guide you.

11. Standard tier height is 10cm (4in) which requires three 2.5cm (1in) layers of cake (k). For 12.5cm (5in) tiers you will need one extra layer taken from a second baked cake.

12. Apply some softened ganache to the base board and press the first layer of cake onto the board (l). I usually place the layer that was top of the baked cake, face down on the board.

13. Soften the ganache in the microwave using short bursts of heating, checking and stirring after each interval. It's very easy to soften too much so be careful. You want a peanut-butter-like consistency, not fully melted. Add in flavouring if required (see Tip below). Mix until thoroughly combined (m).

14. Brush the surface of the layer with simple syrup (n). This will seal the crumb and keep the cake moist. I like to add 10% alcohol to my cooled syrup for flavour and as a preservative. To combine with passionfruit filling, a hint of orange liquor will taste fantastic.

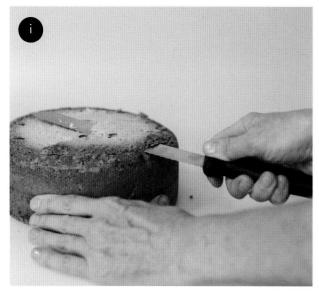

For this example I am using white chocolate ganache as it will allow the added passionfruit flavouring to come through strongly. The cake itself is coconut and pecan, which pairs beautifully with passionfruit. Here I have used a freeze-dried fruit powder which has an amazing clear taste. I use flavourings that will be stable at room temperature such as powders, pastes and oils. Fresh fruits should be used with caution as mould can develop during the preparation time, particularly with whole fruit chunks or berries.

Cakes should be cold during preparation for best results, so keep them in the fridge before ganaching.

15. Use a palette knife to spread a layer of passionfruit ganache over the base layer (o). Gently work the ganache in side-to-side strokes, spreading it outwards and over the edge of the layer. Avoid dragging the ganache inwards as it will incorporate crumb into the ganache. The layer of filling should be around 1cm (½in) thick.

16. Lay the second layer of cake on top (p), then add syrup to that layer and apply another 1cm (½in) layer of passionfruit ganache.

17. Add the final layer of cake (q). Don't apply syrup or add ganache to this one yet, as you need to trim the sides first.

18. Use a serrated knife to trim the sides if necessary. If your baked cake already sits within the perimeter of the cake board, then you may not need to, but most will require some trimming. You are looking for a 5mm–1cm (¼–½in) gap between where the cake finishes and the edge of the cake board. Use a right angle to check (r). Softer cakes may require a thicker layer of ganache, and firmer ones less. A nice thick outside layer of ganache will allow you to get a perfect finish with your fondant.

19. After the sides are trimmed, the top can be brushed with syrup and a ganache layer added. Spread the ganache over the sides of the cake to seal in the crumb (s). For this crumb coat, you can continue with the passionfruit ganache, then as you move onto the final outer layer, you should use plain white chocolate ganache as it will give you a firmer result.

20. Neaten up the ganache with a flat scraper and scrape in any excess at the top edge (t). Make sure no ganache goes beyond the width of the cake board. Refrigerate until the cake is cool to touch.

21. Using unflavoured white chocolate ganache, add a layer to the top surface of cake, extending it out so it forms a 'hat' that is wider than the cake board. Use a scraper to make the top surface as flat and level as possible. With the cake on a turntable, use a long style scraper and keep one side of the scraper roughly at the middle of the cake and the other side skimming the outside edge as the cake spins. Measure points around the edge of the top surface to check the levelness. Add soft ganache to any low points or scrape back any higher points, until the top is perfectly flat (u).

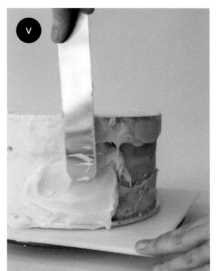

22. Dampen the shiny side of your second cake board and place it face-down on the top surface. Make sure that top and bottom boards are perfectly aligned by using a right-angled ruler or scraper and checking intervals around the cake. Continue to check alignment during the final stages to make sure the top board has not slipped. Start filling the sides with a thick layer of softened ganache (v).

23. Scrape back any excess ganache using a scraper with a blade longer than the cake height Fill any gaps or concave areas with more ganache. As you reach the final stages, it helps to have the ganache at a softer consistency, and skim the scraper around while spinning the turntable (w). I like to add some soft ganache along the blade of the scraper and use that to spread a thin layer evenly around the sides. If this process is taking too long, put the cake back in the fridge to firm it up. The ganache should be firming up quickly as you add the last thin layers.

24. Do a final check of the sides by holding the flat blade against the cake and checking if you can see any light between the scraper and the cake. When there is no gap between the two, the shape is perfect (x).

25. Heat the blade of a fine paring knife by dipping it in boiling water. Wipe it dry then insert it under the top cake board and run it under the entire circumference of the top board. Then use gentle upward pressure to lift off the top board (y).

26. If any ragged edges remain, gently drag them towards the centre of the tier using the flat scraper (z). Dip a finger into hot water and run it around the top edge to do a final smooth of that line.

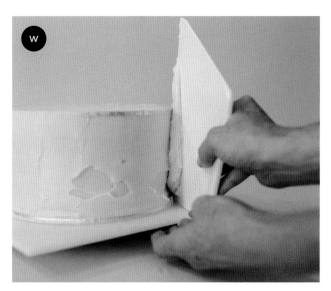

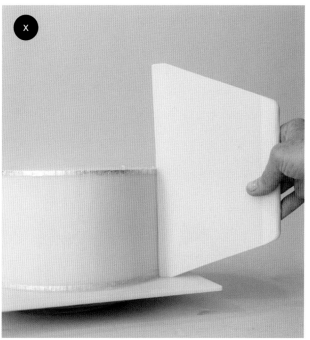

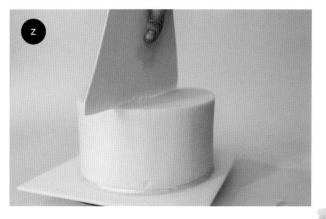

Covering

Once you have prepared your cake with a perfect coat of ganache, you are ready to cover the tiers in fondant. Being meticulous at this stage will give you the ideal canvas for your design, so take your time to get it right.

MATERIALS

- Tiers of cake prepared with ganache
- Base board with centre dowel attached
- Supports such as thin dowel, wooden kebab skewers or straws
- Cutters or secateurs for supports
- Fondant
- Cornflour (cornstarch)
- Rolling pin
- Cake smoothers with straight edge
- Acetate buffers
- Pins and acupuncture needles
- Jam (jelly) syrup
- Pastry brush
- Paring knife
- Modelling tool
- Ganache or royal icing to use as 'glue'

ESTIMATING QUANTITIES OF FONDANT

The table below shows the approximate quantities of fondant you will need to cover a variety of round and square cake sizes, based on a tier height of 10cm (4in). Allowance has been made for the extra fondant required in the rolling process, which will be lost when you trim.

diameter/ width	round cakes	square cakes
10cm (4in)	400g (14oz)	550g (1lb 4oz)
12.5cm (5in)	500g (1lb 2oz)	650g (1lb 7oz)
15cm (6in)	550g (1lb 4oz)	750g (1lb 10oz)
18cm (7in)	750g (1lb 10oz)	900g (2lb)
20cm (8in)	850g (1lb 14oz)	1.1kg (2lb 7½oz)
23cm (9in)	950g (2lb 2oz)	1.25kg (2lb 12oz)
25cm (10in)	1.25kg (2lb 12oz)	1.6kg (3lb 8oz)
28cm (11in)	1.45kg (3lb 3½oz)	1.85kg (4lb 2oz)
30cm (12in)	1.6kg (3lb 8oz)	2.1kg (4lb 11½oz)
33cm (13in)	1.85kg (4lb 2oz)	2.25kg (5lb)
35.5cm (14in)	2.1kg (4lb 11½oz)	2.5kg (5lb 8oz)

1. Cut the required amount of fondant (see Estimating Quantities of Fondant) and begin to kneed it on a clean, cornflour (cornstarch) dusted surface. Fold and press firmly, then rotate the fondant slightly, and repeat folding, pressing and turning until the fondant forms a smooth ball (a).

2. Place the ball with the smooth side facing up and dust it with a little more cornflour (b).

3. Starting at the centre, roll the rolling pin back and forth to flatten the fondant (c).

4. Lift and turn the fondant after every few rolls to prevent it from sticking and to create a regular, rounded shape (d).

5. Stop and pop any air bubbles as you see them (e). Use a regular pin for large bubbles and fine acupuncture needles for smaller ones.

6. When the fondant is rolled to around 5mm (¼in) thickness, skim your rolling pin over the surface to bring up any air bubbles and feel for uneven areas (f). Pop any bubbles and roll over any thicker areas if necessary. Check the diameter with a ruler if you are not used to judging by eye. For this 20cm (8in) cake with 10cm (4in) high sides, the diameter needs to be 20+10+10=40cm (8+4+4=16in) plus a little extra to allow for easier working.

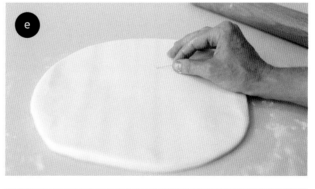

7. Apply jam (jelly) syrup lightly over the ganached cake (g). The jam syrup is made by boiling together a mix of 80% strained or particle free apricot jam (nappage) with 20% water. Allow to cool before using. This thick mixture has good viscosity and prevents the fondant from sliding and wrinkling during the covering process as long as you don't apply too much. It should be a very thin coat, just enough to make the surface sticky.

8. Place your rolling pin at the edge of the fondant and begin rolling it up (h). When most is rolled, you can pick it up and bring the cake to the table.

9. Drape the fondant over the top, trying to keep the cake centred (i). The first step is to push out any air that might be trapped under the top surface by first smoothing with hands and then with a cake smoother. Pop bubbles with a pin if needed.

10. At this point, the sides of the cake will have many folds of excess fondant. The process to smooth out these folds is to pull the folds out while smoothing down the sides of the cake with your hands (j). Work on the side of the cake that's furthest away from you and then work around the cake, stretching out one fold at a time then smoothing it down. You may need to pull out a section that has already been smoothed down to be able to ease down the next fold as you move around.

11. After all folds are smoothed down, run a modelling tool with a soft pointed edge around the base of the cake where the fondant meets the board (k). This will push the fondant right down to the bottom edge and allow you to make a nice clean cut at the bottom.

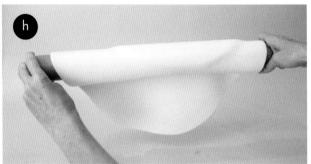

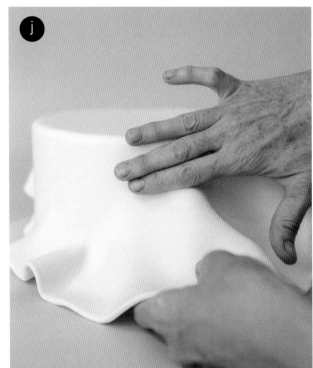

12. Cut off the excess carefully, making sure your knife is angled vertically for the neatest trim (l).

13. Take away and save the excess fondant to re-use, and place the trimmed tier onto a non-slip mat (m).

14. Use a smoother to skim around the sides of the cake (n). At this stage this is just a quick smooth to make sure the fondant is sitting nice and tightly against the ganache.

15. Work the top edge as the first priority and form the sharp edges before the fondant dries and develops a 'skin'. To do this, hold the smoothers so the flat surface of the one at the side meets a straight edge of the one at the top (o). Use firm and directed pressure at the point where the two smoothers meet to force the fondant into the sharp angle. During this process you should be moving the smoothers together in smooth arcs around the top edge of the cake .

16. Most of the work is done with the rigid smoothers, and then you can refine and smooth even more with softer acetate buffers for a flawless finish. These are held the same way as the rigid smoothers when working on the sharp edge. Then when smoothing the sides, use one hand to hold a smoother flat against the cake and polish over the surface (p).

17. A thinner buffer allows you to feel for any air bubbles. Pop these with a pin or acupuncture needle if needed (q). If the ganache you have used underneath is dark chocolate, the way to minimise any dark spots coming through the pin hole is to apply the pin from underneath and at a shallow angle. Any mark will be less visible than if it were pricked straight from the front. I recommend spending quite a bit of time refining the sides with the buffer for the smoothest and most polished result.

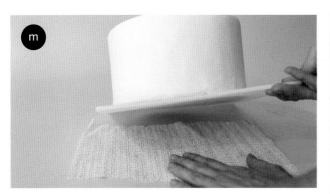

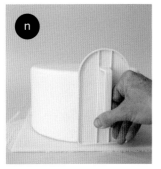

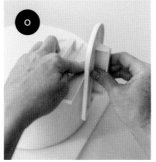

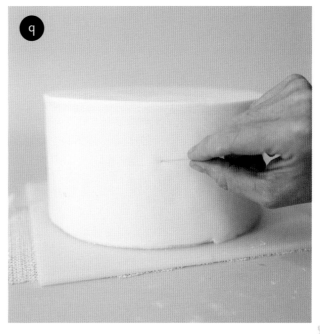

Ideally you should cover a cake with fondant the day after ganaching, so it's very firm and stable. Covering the same day is possible but a little trickier, so use a lighter touch.

Dowelling & stacking

Having covered the cake tiers in fondant, it's now time to stack them securely together. Getting this stage right means the difference between a sturdy construction that doesn't lose its shape when on display, and a teetering tower that may not even survive the journey from your kitchen to its final destination!

1. Stack the cake immediately after covering it, while the fondant is still a little pliable. Begin by applying white chocolate ganache or royal icing to the cake board (a).

2. Lift the bottom tier from underneath and thread it over the centre pole (b). After lowering it onto the board, neaten up the area where the pole has broken through the top surface of the cake. Cut off any excess and push the fondant back so it closes in around the pole. Check if the cake is centred on the board and push with buffers or smoothers if it needs to be moved. Rub over the sides with smoothers and check for any marks or damage from handling. Pay particular attention to the bottom edge and use a smoother to push that down to meet the cake board neatly.

3. Push your supports into the cake (c). For maximum stability, these should be positioned close to where the edge of the next tier will be. If they are too close to the centre, the structure will not support the upper tiers correctly. Measure if necessary to position the supports well. Mark the supports at the point they meet the fondant, then pull them out a little, trim to size and push them back in so they fit flush with the top surface.

4. Apply royal icing or white chocolate ganache to the surface, particularly over the supports. Lower the next tier into place, check the alignment and smooth any marks. Carefully smooth the bottom edge to minimise any gap between the two cakes (d).

5. Repeat the process of dowelling and stacking for any remaining tiers (e). Before putting the top tier in place, check the height of the centre pole to make sure it will be fully covered when the top tier is in its final position.

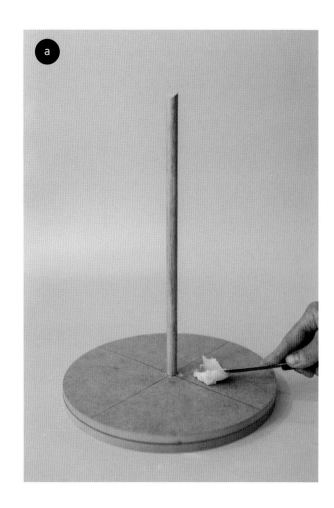

a

Finishing

It's all in the finishing! The final detailing will complete the foundations of your cake, giving it a tailored and sleek look. Neat finishing can draw the eye away from small imperfections and results in a more unified look. I prefer to cover the cake board after stacking. It can either be done the day prior to decorating or as one of the final steps after the cake sides have been decorated.

MATERIALS

- White fondant
- Cake board the same size as bottom tier of cake
- Ribbons
- Pins
- Smoothers and buffers

1. For covering a cake board, the fondant should be rolled thinner than you would have it to cover the cake. Around 2–3mm (1/16–1/8in) is good. When it is rolled to a size larger than the cake board to be covered, cut a hole in the centre the same size as the bottom tier, using a tier cake board as a template (a).

2. Remove the circle and make a cut to the back of the fondant (b).

3. Fold back the sides of the fondant, bring in the cake, orient it so it is facing to the front, and wrap the fondant around the base. On a larger cake board, you can put the fondant in place before adding water to secure it, but for a board with only a very small edge like this one, wet first and then add the fondant (c). If adding the water after positioning, lift the sides of the fondant and tuck the brush underneath to add the water.

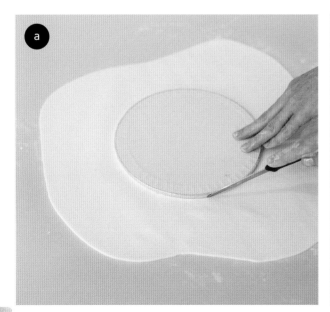

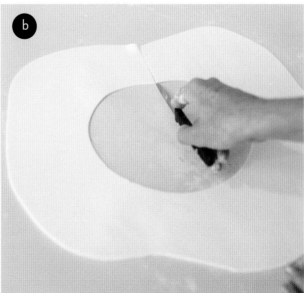

4. At the back, there will probably be an overlap where the fondant has stretched a little. Trim this so the ends meet neatly (d).

5. Use an acetate buffer to smooth over the seam (e). If you get to this quickly, it's possible to polish it to a point where the seam is invisible.

6. Roughly trim off the excess fondant at the edge of the cake board, then use a small scraper to do a more refined trim at the board edge. Start with the scraper flat against the board and then curve it down so it pushes the fondant towards the edge of the board and trims the excess, creating a smooth curve at the board edge (f). Work quickly around the board and then use an acetate buffer to do a final smooth and polish around the board.

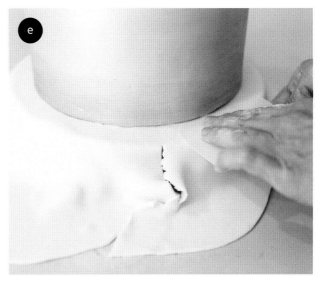

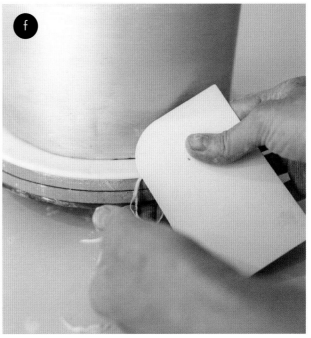

7. To attach a ribbon trim to the base board, double-sided tape is most effective. Apply the tape around the board, starting at the back and then peel away the backing tape. Next carefully apply the ribbon, again starting at the back. Be very careful that it stays in a straight line. It helps to be at eye level during this step. Leave a small overlap at the back and trim the excess by cutting the ribbon on an angle. A small dot of hot glue or double-sided tape can be used to secure the overlap if needed (g).

8. To trim the tiers with ribbon, first decide where the join will be. If you will be adding a feature bow (see Tying a Bow), the join can be at the front and will be covered up. Otherwise the join can be at the back or in a place where it will be covered by flowers or decorations. Pin one end in place and wrap the ribbon around the tier (h).

9. Cut the ribbon to size leaving a small overlap. Pull it taut and add a tiny dot of hot glue on the overlap, then press that firmly against the end of the ribbon that is pinned to the cake (i). Remove the pin.

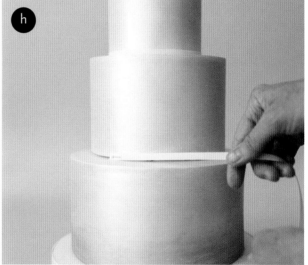

If the bottom edge of your cake is not perfect, the ribbon will not sit neatly. You may need to trim off any excess bumps of fondant or fill any gaps between the tiers. To fill gaps, paint on a little piping gel and then push in some kneaded fondant. Trim with a sharp knife and buff smooth with an acetate buffer.

TYING A BOW

10. Pinch a small loop of ribbon from a long length (j).

11. Take the long end behind the loop, and then across the top of the loop (k).

12. Still working with the long end of the ribbon, push a second loop through the underside of the knot you just created (l).

13. Pull and tweak the loops and ends until the bow looks neat and regular (m).

14. Trim the ends on an angle (n). I like the look of a cut with the longer end on the inside and shorter end on the outside.

15. Secure over the ribbon join using hot glue (o).

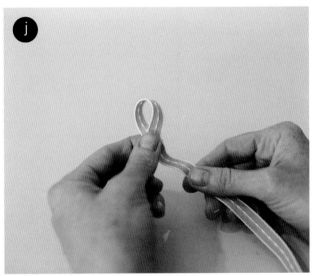

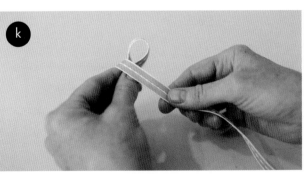

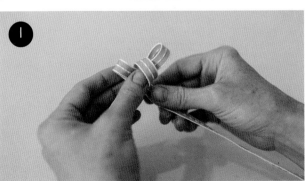

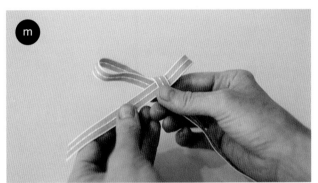

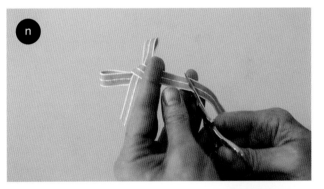

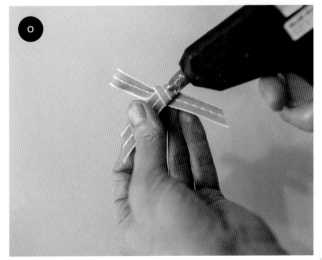

Templates

Templates are shown at full size. You can download printable versions of these templates from http://ideas.sewandso.co.uk/patterns.

GOLDEN
REGENCY

Frame

GOLDEN REGENCY

Loop and leaf motif

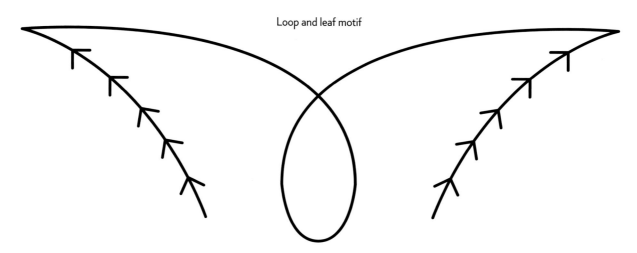

Suppliers

AUSTRALIA

Cakers Warehouse
4/48 Shandan Circuit
Albion Park Rail
NSW 2527
+61 02 4256 9285
and at
15/118-126 Princes Highway
Fairy Meadow
NSW 2519
+61 02 4285 1927
www.cakerswarehouse.com.au
All general and specialised supplies,
ingredients, boards, boxes, edible lustre,
isomalt, cutters, moulds, tools, dragees,
stencils, fondant

Bakels
33 Derby St
Silverwater
NSW 2128
+61 02 9739 9300
www.bakels.com.au
Ready to Roll Pettinice (fondant),
ingredients such as sugar, pure icing and
glycerine

Faye Cahill Cake Design
104 Addison Rd
Marrickville
NSW 2204
+61 02 9568 3165
www.fayecahill.com.au
Stencils, cutters, cake stands, edible lustre

The Gold Leaf Factory
Factory #3 / 26 Moresby Avenue
Seaford
Victoria 3198
+61 03 9786 2247
Edible gold and silver leaf transfer sheets,
loose leaf, flakes and sprinkles

UK

Cake Stuff
Milton Industrial Estate
Lesmahagow
ML11 0JN
www.cake-stuff.com
All general supplies and tools, colours,
lustres, ingredients and specialty items

Cake Craft Company
Unit 13-14
Muirhead Quay
Fresh Wharf Estate
Barking
IG11 7BG
+44 203 637 4715
www.cakecraftcompany.com
All general supplies and tools, colours,
lustres, ingredients and specialty items

USA

Sunflower Sugar Art
6001 Highway A1A
PMB 8102
Indian River Shores
FL 32963
+1 772 217 2897
www.sunflowersugarart.com
Petal dusts, cutters, veiners,
impression mats

Sugar Delites
405 E. Kott Rd.
Manistee
MI 49660
+1 231 723 5774
www.sugardelites.com
Botanically correct cutters and veiners

About the author

Faye Cahill has been a professional cake decorator for over 20 years. Her company, Faye Cahill Cake Design, is based in Sydney, Australia, and recently passed the milestone of 11 years in business.

Faye is a wedding specialist and was named wedding cake decorator of the year for 2015 at the international Cake Masters awards. She was also awarded wedding cake decorator of the year for 2017 by The Australian Cake Decorating Network. Among the many thousands of cakes Faye has made over her career have been cakes for celebrities and high-profile events, film, tv, advertisements. Her work has featured in many fashion and wedding magazines and blogs. Faye's design aesthetic pairs tailored, refined looks with fine detailing and stylised flowers. She has been sharing her craft through teaching and tutorials for almost 10 years and teaches efficient methods suitable for both commercial work and sugarcraft enthusiasts. Teaching credits include guest teaching at schools in France, Spain, Germany, Indonesia, Malaysia, USA, UK, UAE, Dominican Republic and Switzerland as well as private teaching in Bahamas and Thailand. Faye offers two online classes with Craftsy and several downloadable PDF tutorials.

Faye is a brand ambassador for Bakels Pettinice fondant as well as Cakers Warehouse supply store. Through her own company she offers a range of products including edible lustres and sugarcraft stencils. *The Gilded Cake* is Faye's first book.

THANKS

Deepest thanks to the wonderful team at F&W Media International for this incredible opportunity. To Ame Verso for trusting me with this concept and guiding me through the process, Jeni Hennah and Jane Trollope for your careful and precise editing of my words, and Sam Staddon for the beautiful design and layouts.

I would like to thank the wonderful cake community for endless support and encouragement. To all those who follow my work on social media, take the time to like and interact with my posts – you give me the affirmation I need to keep working and striving to be better. To all those who have attended a class or learnt with me through an online tutorial, thank you for the opportunity to travel, teach and meet so many of my fellow cakers. I could never have imagined that this career would take me so many places and bring me so many wonderful friends throughout the world.

To my closest industry friends who I have worked alongside, learnt from and been inspired by. Thank you for your friendship and encouraging words: Jacqueline Butler, Stevi Auble, Miso Bakes, Jacinta Perkins, Gillian Brown, Lorinda Rogers, Sharon Wee, Margie Carter, Chris Chavez, Michelle Pattinson, Daniel Dieguez, Paul Bradford, David Brice, Erin Schwartz, Joey Mariano and a special mention to Jean Michel Raynaud who influenced and changed the way I approach design.

To my clients who trust us to make the cake for their milestone events. The wedding and event planners, the many venues that recommend us and our talented event industry friends.

To my amazing team at Faye Cahill Cake Design who make the impossible possible. Some who have stayed with me for many years and some who have passed through. Thanks for being so creative, loyal, trustworthy and solid under pressure. Thanks for your company, advice, laughs and inspiration: Mavournee Georgeson, Viola Bechara, Maree Cahill, Rebecca Greenberg, Lauren Croghan, Jane Tan, Hugo Rocha, Fernanda Pieranti, Theresa Tran, Janyn Chua, Katie Veile and Jade Moore.

To Lucy Leonardi, who has shot many beautiful images for me, including those in this book. Thank you for your wonderful eye for detail, light and composition, and for being such a pleasure to work with.

To my wonderful designer Paola Pelligro who designed my beautiful logo and website.

To my family, especially my wonderful creative, smart, funny and beautiful daughter Ramona.

Index

A SEWANDSO BOOK
© F&W Media International, Ltd 2018

SewandSo is an imprint of F&W Media International, Ltd
Pynes Hill Court, Pynes Hill, Exeter, EX2 5AZ, UK

F&W Media International, Ltd is a subsidiary of F+W Media, Inc
10151 Carver Road, Suite #200, Blue Ash, OH 45242, USA

Text and Designs © Faye Cahill 2018
Layout and Photography © F&W Media International, Ltd 2018

First published in the UK and USA in 2018

A catalogue record for this book is available from the British Library.

ISBN-13: 978-1-4463-0711-3 paperback
SRN: R7786 paperback

ISBN-13: 978-1-4463-7667-6 PDF
SRN: R7961 PDF

ISBN-13: 978-1-4463-7666-9 EPUB
SRN: R7960 EPUB

Printed in China by RR Donnelley for:
F&W Media International, Ltd
Pynes Hill Court, Pynes Hill, Exeter, EX2 5AZ, UK

10 9 8 7 6 5 4 3 2 1

Content Director: Ame Verso
Managing Editor: Jeni Hennah
Project Editor: Jane Trollope
Proofreader: Cheryl Brown
Design Manager: Lorraine Inglis
Designer: Sam Staddon
Photographer: Lucy Leonardi
Production Manager: Beverley Richardson

F&W Media publishes high quality books on a wide range of subjects.
For more great book ideas visit: www.sewandso.co.uk

Layout of the digital edition of this book may vary depending on reader hardware and display settings.